In the same series:

LEONID ANDREYEV *Josephine M. Newcombe*
ISAAC BABEL *R. W. Hallett*
SIMONE DE BEAUVOIR *Robert Cottrell*
SAUL BELLOW *Brigitte Scheer-Schäzler*
BERTOLT BRECHT *Willy Haas*
ALBERT CAMUS *Carol Petersen*
WILLA CATHER *Dorothy Tuck McFarland*
COLETTE *Robert Cottrell*
JULIO CORTÁZAR *Evelyn Picon Garfield*
JOHN DOS PASSOS *George J. Becker*
THEODORE DREISER *James Lundquist*
FRIEDRICH DÜRRENMATT *Armin Arnold*
T. S. ELIOT *Joachim Seyppel*
WILLIAM FAULKNER *Joachim Seyppel*
MAX FRISCH *Carol Petersen*
ROBERT FROST *Elaine Barry*
MAKSIM GORKI *Gerhard Habermann*
GÜNTER GRASS *Kurt Lothar Tank*
PETER HANDKE *Nicholas Hern*
ERNEST HEMINGWAY *Samuel Shaw*
HERMANN HESSE *Franz Baumer*
UWE JOHNSON *Mark Boulby*
JAMES JOYCE *Armin Arnold*
FRANZ KAFKA *Franz Baumer*
SINCLAIR LEWIS *James Lundquist*
GEORG LUKÁCS *Ehrhard Bahr and Ruth Goldschmidt Kunzer*
THOMAS MANN *Arnold Bauer*
CARSON MCCULLERS *Richard M. Cook*
ALBERTO MORAVIA *Jane E. Cottrell*
VLADIMIR NABOKOV *Donald E. Morton*
EUGENE O'NEILL *Horst Frenz*
JOSÉ ORTEGA Y GASSET *Franz Niedermayer*
GEORGE ORWELL *Roberta Kalechofsky*
KATHERINE ANNE PORTER *John Edward Hardy*
EZRA POUND *Jeannette Lander*
MARCEL PROUST *James R. Hewitt*
RAINER MARIA RILKE *Arnold Bauer*
JEAN-PAUL SARTRE *Liselotte Richter*
UPTON SINCLAIR *Jon Yoder*
ISAAC BASHEVIS SINGER *Irving Malin*
THORNTON WILDER *Hermann Stresau*
THOMAS WOLFE *Fritz Heinrich Ryssel*
VIRGINIA WOOLF *Manly Johnson*
RICHARD WRIGHT *David Bakish*

Modern Literature Monographs

General Editor: Lina Mainiero

S. Y. AGNON

Harold Fisch

Frederick Ungar Publishing Co.
New York

Printed in the United States of America
Library of Congress Catalog Card No.: 74-76126
Designed by Anita Duncan
ISBN: 0-8044-2197-8

(This book incorporates ideas developed in two earlier essays by Harold Fisch: "Agnon's Tales of Mystery and Imagination," *Tradition,* IX (1967), pp. 123–37 and "The Dreaming Narrator in S. Y. Agnon," *Novel,* IV (1970), pp. 49–68.)

Contents

Chronology

1888: Born Shmuel Yosef Czaczkes in Buczacz, Galicia.

1891: Attended infant school (*heder*).

1894: Began more formal studies at home under direction of his father, a fur merchant. Mainly Jewish classical texts.

1900: Studied in the local *Bet Midrash* (House of Study) under the direction of Rabbi Shmuel Yisakhar Shtark, a distinguished scholar.

1903: Began publishing poems in the Hebrew and Yiddish press.

1906: Became assistant editor of a Yiddish weekly.

1907: Moved to Lwow (Lemberg) where he continued editing and writing. After some months, with the failure of the Hebrew weekly, *Ha'Et,* he made the journey overland to Trieste where he embarked for Palestine, arriving in Jaffa May 2, 1907.

1908: First Jaffa story, *Agunot,* published. Adopted name of Agnon.

1911: Settled in Jerusalem.

1912: Achieved acclaim with the publication of *Vehaya He'Akov LeMishor (And the Crooked Shall Be Made Straight)*. Friendship with Y. H. Brenner.

1913: Left for Berlin. Began acquaintance with several major Jewish writers.

1916: Spent several months in hospital with kidney disease.

1920: Married Esther Marx.

1921: Moved to Homburg. Daughter, Emuna, born.

1922: Birth of son, Hemdat.

1924: Homburg house gutted by fire. Library of books and manuscripts destroyed, also unfinished novel. Returned to Palestine where he was later joined by his family. Settled in Jerusalem.

1929: His home in Talpiot, Jerusalem, plundered by Arabs. Books and papers destroyed.

1930: Made a sentimental journey to his home town in Galicia.

1954: Received Israel Prize for Literature. (Awarded him a second time in 1958.)

1966: Nobel Prize for Literature. (Shared with poetess, Nelly Sachs.)

1967: Visited the United States.

1970: Died.

1971: Posthumous publication of *Shira,* an unfinished novel.

1

Introduction

In his brief autobiographical statement made at the State Banquet in Stockholm on receiving the Nobel Prize for Literature in December 1966, Agnon declared that though he was born in Buczacz in Galicia it always seemed to him as though he had been born in Jerusalem. In the same speech he declared that his direct literary progenitors were the authors of the Hebrew Scriptures, and that according to his family tradition he was a Levite descended from the singers and poets of the Temple. To them he claims to belong, using their language—Hebrew—and following their traditions. Agnon's tone is always slightly playful, and the speech at Stockholm was no exception. He enjoyed teasing his auditors just as he teases the readers of his novels by darting to and fro across the border between fact and fantasy. In one of his lighter tales *BiLevav Yamin*, 1935 (*In the Heart of the Seas*), in which he incidentally also identifies himself by name, he has his hero make the journey from Buczacz to Jerusalem riding on a kerchief. But this is not merely a case of oriental fantasy. To understand Agnon correctly, we have to understand the telescoping of time and place as a basic ingredient of his imagination.

The fact is that for a pious Jew like Agnon, brought up in eastern Galicia at the end of the nineteenth century, Maimonides, Judah the Prince, and King David are his contemporaries. There is a simultaneity about the Jewish learning and experience of all the ages. This is not a matter of escapism: one does not seek refuge in the classical sources of Judaism—the *Torah*—from the harsh realities of the environment. On the contrary, the whole corpus of biblical rabbinic and hasidic literature, that corpus which Agnon began to absorb from infancy, is felt as directly and urgently relevant to life in the here and now. And if half the laws, the tales and the poetry refer to the Land of Israel, that makes them no less relevant. A flick of the page and we find ourselves in the *Song of Songs* among the flora and fauna of a remembered landscape. It is nearer to one than the fir forest outside the town because it is more interior, and also because it is more concrete. More connected with folklore and ritual like the citron and the palm used in the celebration of the feast of Tabernacles.

Agnon, who had been brought up in this tradition of piety, was a scholar amongst scholars. He moved with ease over the vast literature of early and late Hebrew texts. His collection of four thousand books, many of them both rare and ancient, was destroyed by fire in Germany in 1924, but by the time of his death he had amassed an even greater collection in his home in Jerusalem. Never has there been a novelist who lived to this extent in the world of books. With poets, it is possible to point to a Dante, a Goethe, or a Milton—all of them writers whose imaginations were seemingly fired by the written word accumulated from the past. Not so with novelists. We are accustomed to think of them as drawing directly from the life around them, distilling their word from the experience of every day. With Agnon it is somewhat different. Certainly his work reflects the ongoing processes of Jewish life in his time. It has frequently been termed an epic of modern Jewish history, but his tone is scholarly and meditative. Character and event are beheld in a context which is fundamentally literary. When the wife of Daniel Bach

---

All passages cited are from the Hebrew texts, and are translated by the present author, except where otherwise stated. See "Notes" on pp. 109–113. A list of major English translations of Agnon's books is given in the Bibliography.

in *A Guest for the Night* returns home from Austria to Galicia at the end of the First World War, she does so because like everyone else, she imagined that now the sword of battle had rested and the days of the Messiah would come. But, adds the narrator, "the Messiah was still binding and loosening his wounds and the world had not yet returned to a state of health."[1] The image of the sick and wounded Messiah, son of David, sitting at the gate of Rome because the world is not yet ready to be redeemed is drawn from a rabbinic legend recounted in the Babylonian *Talmud* and elsewhere. Here again there is the dissolution of history in a framework of literary reminiscence. All the wars are one war; all the exiles are one exile.

Literary allusion is also a major source of irony. In a later chapter, the legless Daniel Bach says to his father, "The Wars of Gog and Magog have been and gone, but there is yet no sign of the Messiah"—the point being that according to the prophet Ezekiel[2] the two events ought to follow closely on one another. But Daniel Bach's conclusion is not entirely borne out by the novel. In this very meeting with Daniel Bach and his father, the narrator has just been giving the latter instructions regarding the route from Jaffa to Ramat Rahel, a village near Jerusalem. The Messiah has not yet come, but the journey of Reb Shlomo Bach to the Land of Israel takes on, in the context of the novel, a quasi-messianic significance. It is the natural sequel to the Wars of Gog and Magog. Such biblical and Talmudic echo does not need to be explained because it is part of a literary tradition which Agnon shares with his audience.

The peculiarly "literary" character of Agnon's style is also part of this same evocation of a shared and compendious tradition. The savoring of language, the use of literary echo, unexpected twists of familiar phraseology and constant wordplay suggest a kind of verbal creativity which we do not normally associate with the novel—at least not since the early novels of the Elizabethan period in England. The critic Ian Watt has taught us that with the rise of the more modern novel, language is used as "a purely referential medium" rather than as a source of interest in its own right.[3] This would evidently not apply to Agnon and other Hebrew writers of his generation. At a time when Hebrew writers were just beginning to fashion a new instrument of prose out of the extraordinary variety of traditional styles, there was fun in simply doing finger-exercises with Hebrew. Neologisms were a popular topic of conversation. One was expected to savor language and take pleasure in its coloration, its cultivated elegance and wit. Nor was this a matter of a narrow or upper class literary culture. Quite the contrary. Agnon's self-conscious literary skill, and his stylistic virtuosity first established his popularity with all ranks and classes of the new Hebrew-reading public. It happened with the publication in Jaffa of his story *Agunot*. The story's opening sentences immediately announced the hand of the master:

It has been said that through the doings of Israel there runs a thread of grace and that the Holy One Blessed is He, in person, sits down and uses it to weave an endless *Tallit* [prayer shawl] of perfect beauty with which the Congregation of Israel might wrap itself! So that she can go on shining and glowing, beautiful as ever even in these times of exile just as she was in her youth, in her father's house, in that royal temple and that royal city. And when the Blessed One sees that she hasn't, Heaven forbid, been marked or stained by her stay in the lands of her enemies, He, so to speak, gives an approving nod of the head and launches into her praises, saying: "Behold thou art fair, my bride; behold, thou art fair." (*Song of Songs*, I, 15)[4]

This euphuism or "high" style is more noticeable in the earlier and simpler stories. Of the longer novels it is characteristic of *A Bridal Canopy*, a work of epic scope but of relatively simple conception. Interestingly, as the story line becomes more contorted, the style seems to get simpler. His highly esoteric *Book of Fables* (discussed in chapter 6, pp. 68–83) contains some of the simplest writing in the canon.

Agnon's Hebrew style has been the subject of much discussion. Some have claimed that it is molded on the cadences of Yiddish—the everyday language among the Jews of eastern Europe.[5] Obviously Agnon spoke Yiddish; indeed some of his juvenile stories and essays were written in that tongue. And in his mature novels he often seems to be translating from Yiddish in the conversational passages. But the fundamental style of his novels is, I would say, much more closely related to the Hebrew of the *Midrash*, i.e., the classical rabbinic homily of the early middle ages, than to the Yiddish spoken in his environment, as in the passage quoted above with its chiseled midrashic phraseology. But in spite of the mannered, ornate style, we have the feeling constantly that the author has us by the hand, or rather by the coat-lapel, and is speaking directly into our ear. This is an achievement probably not of style but of literary personality. In every line we sense an ever-present literary-narrative personality whose tone is unwavering, and who has the gift of holding our attention even when he is uttering seeming banalities or building up mandarin structures of artificial image and phrase.

In spite of the extraordinary variety of style and

manner, Agnon's tone is constant. Throughout the novels there is one single voice, one mediating literary personality whose tone we quickly learn to recognize. It is, as we have already noted, often playful and whimsical. But this tone of playfulness is bound up with something else—the quality of seeming to hold something always in reserve, of having some further knowledge which he means still to impart. He teases us with a sense of mystery. It is a quiet tone, moreover; Agnon never preaches, never shouts, and never argues, but he is always "there." His writing has for this reason been termed lyrical. But the term is misleading. If he never lets us forget his presence, this does not mean he is writing of himself. The story is always uppermost, never the storyteller. It is a story of endless invention, like the thread of grace with which the Holy One—he tells us—spins out the story of his people. In relation to his fiction, Agnon does in fact preside rather like the divine providence of Jewish tradition. He is someone who "knows," and whose tale will go on forever. Above all, someone who sees and is not seen, a pervasive rather than an intrusive presence who lets his characters act out their own destinies. If we dislike this voice and this presence, we had better leave Agnon alone because it is impossible to appreciate Agnon's novels without appreciating the narrative personality—the voice through which they are mediated.

What are Agnon's stories about? His style is bookish but he is not really writing about books. His manner is personal, subjective, but it is not his own story he tells. His subject ultimately is people. There are hundreds of them in his writings—a teeming population of rich and astounding variety. Perhaps the ultimate gift of a true storyteller is this fertility in the production of a multitude of characters and events. Agnon has this kind of fertility to a high degree. He is a compulsive storyteller with always another tale pushing on the heels of the one presently in hand. Where do all the tales come from—the hundreds of stories and the thousands of secondary tales within those stories? Of course, such invention is a quality of imagination. It is what the great novelists, Dickens, Gogol, Balzac, possess so magnificently. It is what makes a fictional artist. But true invention is fed also from observation of people and their doings. Henry James tells us how the germs of his novels came from some dinner-table scrap of conversation, a fleeting glance of a man or a woman with just the minimum of information about their histories. *What Maisie Knew* was born from the accidental mention of a luckless child of a divorced couple who is tossed to and fro between her parents and their new spouses. From this scrap of living tissue he developed the whole subtle organism of the novel. This is the manner of fictional invention. Agnon's tales are more solidly anchored than those of Henry James in living character and situation. Though he denied ever writing a *roman à clef*, there can be no doubt that he is often glancing at people he knew, and in some of the novels one can actually identify characters and episodes from his wide circle of acquaintances. He was always as deeply involved with people as with books.

In the aforementioned speech delivered at Stockholm on December 10, 1966, Agnon related how on his arrival in Jaffa in 1907 he had become secretary of the local Jewish court and, subsequently, of the Land of Israel Council—the parliament in embryo of the Jewish settlers throughout the land. In this capacity he believed he had come to know every Jewish man, woman, and child in the country. It is a remarkable claim but not entirely incredible when one considers how small the community was at that time, and how it was concentrated in three or four small urban centers and half a dozen villages. The *kibbutzim* had not yet come into existence. There is no doubt that Agnon had an extraordinary capacity for getting to know people and their background, and for picking up their stories. It is this capacity which gives his writings after his arrival in Jaffa in 1907, their epic density and human richness. If the period in Galicia where Agnon spent the first nineteen years of his life gave him his experience of books, the Jaffa period from 1907 to 1913 gave him his experience of people, and it is notable that in his later writing, especially in his great novel *The Day Before Yesterday*, he reverts to the Jaffa period as a major source of human interest.

From an artistic point of view, the move to Palestine was in fact immensely rewarding. The Jewish community, or *Yishuv*, which Agnon found there during the years before the First World War provided ideal material for a novelist on the watch for people and stories. The people of Jaffa, Petah-Tikva, Jerusalem, Rishon LeZion and the other Jewish settlements in Palestine had come from all parts of the world. There he found Jews of the East and West, speaking a variety of tongues. There were upper classes and lower classes: grove-owners as well as indigent workers; both the pious and the unbelievers—the latter gradually gaining the ascendancy during this period of the Second (socialist) Aliyah from 1908 to 1913. This *aliyah* (or wave of immigration) brought some forty thousand young Jews to the Land, many of them from the Ukraine and other parts of Russia. They were on the whole borne on the tide of revolutionary socialist idealism, and their ideas were important in laying the foundation of the future social and economic structure of the country.

Agnon was close to them but not actually of them. He had at least as much sympathy with the older, more traditionally-minded settlers who belonged to the indigenous Jewish population dating back long before the Zionist period. At all events there was here a human landscape as colored and as varied as any novelist could wish for, and the tensions between the different sections, especially between believers and unbelievers, were going to feed the drama of his later work. It was a land in which young men and women were beginning to discover their identity. They were there to start a new life but it was not always possible to break with old obligations and memories. This is the background, for instance, of the delicately poetic tale *Betrothed* set in Jaffa during the years before the First World War.

Agnon left Jaffa for Germany in 1913 intending to stay only for a short time, but owing to the outbreak of the war and the unsettled conditions which ensued in Palestine—actually one of the war zones—Agnon remained in Germany for eleven years. This period from 1913–1924 was as critical for his development as a writer, as were the two earlier periods. By the time he reached Germany he was already a young Hebrew writer of note and he found himself welcomed in literary and intellectual circles. At this period, Germany was the center of Jewish intellectual life. Agnon came to know Martin Buber, Gershom Scholem, Franz Rosenzweig and other scholars, as well as the lay leaders of the community. In Königsberg he met and married Esther Marx, the highly educated daughter of a wealthy and cultivated family very prominent in the affairs of the Jewish community. Germany was a center of Hebrew writers also, some of them in exile like himself. He had contact with the poets Chaim Nahman

Bialik and Jacob Fichman, and with the prominent Hebrew essayist, Ahad Ha'am (Asher Ginzberg). It was a stimulating environment and gave Agnon something he could not have acquired either in eastern Galicia or in Jaffa, namely, the intellectual stimulation of modern scholarship and culture. Agnon found himself mixing freely and on terms of equality with men whose minds had been shaped by German philosophy and western science. He was encouraged to make himself a man of the world, and there is no doubt that during this period he voraciously read contemporary European literature, especially French, German and Russian, acquiring a degree of intellectual maturity comparable to that of major European writers such as Franz Kafka and Thomas Mann. In his later writings he retains the personality and manner of an unsophisticated Galician Yeshiva-student. But this *persona* should not deceive us. It is his way of telling a tale. (Though in some tales, notably in *Shira,* his posthumous novel dealing with the academic community of Jerusalem in the twenties and thirties, the full intellectual range is revealed.) In Germany he also acquired a patron, the philanthropist and publisher Salman Schocken. Schocken, realizing Agnon's achievements and promise, provided him with a life annuity to enable him to write. His publishing house, which later transferred to Tel-Aviv, became the publishers of Agnon's writings. The New York branch of Schocken Books publishes the chief English translations of Agnon.

In 1924, Agnon returned to Jerusalem settling in his home in the Talpiot district where he remained, except for brief visits to Europe and one visit to America, until the time of his death in 1970. There is no doubt that the two geographical poles on which his imagination turned are Buczacz and Jerusalem. He looks also at times to Berlin, but that city does not have the same radical significance for him as the other two. Buczacz is often referred to in the novels under the name of *Shebush* meaning in Hebrew "confusion," whilst Jerusalem (*Yerushalayim*) has the inevitable connotation of peace and perfection. The movement from *Shebush* to *Yerushalayim* is thus a movement from the confusion and the frustration of exile to the wholeness and ease of redemption. But this would be far too simple a scheme of metaphysical geography, for the fact is that in Jerusalem, the Jerusalem of disturbance and riots in the 1920s and 1930s, Agnon dreams of the peace and pious calm of Shebush. The old *Bet Midrash* (House of Prayer and Study) becomes a symbol of a spiritual tranquillity which it is no longer easy to achieve. Conversely, when in Shebush, he dreams of Jerusalem. In fact it seems that only in Shebush can he find the real Jerusalem of perfection and peace! The result is an uneasy movement between the two, sometimes actually dramatized as a journey between the two towns, as in *A Guest for the Night*.

The ultimate question to which Agnon's writing addresses itself is: How is one to mediate between Shebush and Jerusalem, between the past and the present, between nation-building and the pieties of old-world hasidism, between God and socialism, between vision and reality? These are the questions which haunt Agnon's fiction. And they are on the whole unanswered questions. Instead of answers he provides us with fables: the fable, for instance, of the key of the old *Bet Midrash* in Shebush which the narrator brings back with him to Jerusalem to keep as a souvenir and as a pledge for the future. Such fables are often arcane and ambiguous, but they are the only terms on which

Agnon is prepared to discuss with us the ultimate conclusions and significances of his fiction. They invite us into what may be termed the metaphysical level of his artwork, the level at which he attempts to comprehend imaginatively the meaning of Jewish history.

It is possible to enjoy his work—as many readers do—without feeling more than a tremor of metaphysical interest; to enjoy it simply as a rich body of invention, a gallery of people and their doings, and of places we have known either at first sight or by report, but which he actualizes for us more vividly than we can, even by the evidence of our own senses. For the thoughtful reader, however, the ultimate challenge is that of the deeper plot and the deeper resonance: the story of a people and its fate; a story told, so to speak, in the mind of God.

2

The Abandoned Wife

Agnon was born Shmuel Yosef Czaczkes. He adopted the name Agnon with the publication in 1908 of his successful short story *Agunot*. An *aguna* (plural *agunot*) is a woman who in Jewish law is unable to remarry because she is still legally attached to her first husband who has left her without giving her a divorce. By extension it comes to refer to souls of men and women who are separated from their true partners or from their true spiritual homes. Perhaps the correct translation would be "the alienated," except that the Hebrew word suggests a more complex state, something between wholeness and disruption, between marriage and divorce. One relationship is as yet unformed and the other is as yet undissolved. It is a state of radical ambiguity. It was with a fine insight that Agnon chose this term as the linguistic root of his own name, for there can be no question that the *aguna*-motif is central to his writings. His concern is with a world and a community of *agunot*.

The story *Agunot* has a fairy-tale quality. It tells of the beautiful daughter of a wealthy man in Jerusalem who is promised in marriage to an accomplished scholar from Poland. She falls in love, however, with the artist Ben-Uri who has been commissioned by her father to build a holy ark for a synagogue. The result is that Dina will be truly married neither to the one nor to the other. Instead both she and Ben-Uri will go separately into exile and wander the world in a hopeless search, each for his soul's-partner. The story, brief though it is, is many layered, the theme of *agunot* being re-echoed in the lives of all the characters. The scholar to whom Dina's father has betrothed her is also a lost soul. His real love is Fredele, a simple girl from his village in Poland, but she will be married to another. The key to these multiple separations is provided by the quotations from *Song of Songs* which occur throughout this tale. Dina, asleep on her bed at night "whilst her heart is awake," is the *Shulammite* of *Song of Songs* 5: 2. Like the *Shulammite*, her lover too will disappear in the night not to be found. It should be noted that the *Shulammite* is traditionally a symbol for Israel, and the *Song* is the story of her union with God. In the opening sentence of Agnon's tale (quoted on pp. 5–6), the words from the *Song*, "Behold thou art fair, my bride; behold, thou art fair," are applied openly and directly to Israel as the spouse of God; the *Tallit*, or prayer shawl, which he weaves of the doings of Israel being expressive of this love-relation. In the continuation of that passage we hear of the tearing of the *Tallit*, i.e., the disruption of the relationship, and this sets the mood and provides the key for the main idea of the tale, the idea of the *aguna:*

But sometimes, woe betide us, something happens to break the thread. Then the *Tallit* is spoiled and rough winds toss it about and tear it. At once we all feel the sense of shame and we know that we are naked—the Sabbath day is violated, our feast is turned to horror, and our glory to ashes. Then it is that the Congregation of Israel wanders about in her grief and cries out: "The watchmen who went about the city have found me, they have struck me, and wounded me; they have taken away my veil from me." (*Song* 5:7.) Her beloved has turned away and is gone and she looks for him and moans, saying, "If you find my beloved tell him that I am sick for love." (Ibid., verses 6, 8.) And this sickness, woe betide us, brings with it a deep melancholy which will continue until He above pours out his spirit upon us and we repent and achieve those deeds which do us glory and which will again help to spin that thread of grace and love of which we have spoken.[1]

The separation of the lovers is therefore rooted in a greater historical theme, the exile and separation of the People of Israel from its land and from its divine partner. This will explain why Dina and her father, as well as Ben-Uri and the local rabbi of Agnon's tale, have to leave the Holy City—the latter on a mission of "finding a remedy for *agunot*."[2] They are enacting symbolically the theme of exile, and their sadness blends with the poignant memory of the destruction of the Temple, and of Jewish national existence.

Separation and longing are basic ingredients of Agnon's narrative world. In this sense he is an elegiac writer. It is the theme of his earliest and latest writings. His novel *Shira* tells of a man inwardly estranged from his wife, but unable to establish a normal relation with the other woman to whom he is drawn. The earliest poem which he remembers having written in infancy was one of longing for his father during a period of the latter's absence from home. The theme of absent fathers (or husbands) was a commonplace of Jewish writing at this period in eastern Europe, perhaps because so many fathers had to leave home to make long journeys in order to earn a livelihood. But the theme has clear metaphysical overtones also, for the absent father suggests the absent Lord of Jewish history, who leaves his wife or child, i.e., the Jewish people, bereft of his spiritual authority. It is impossible to escape such metaphysical hints. In a more mysterious sense, the *aguna* theme suggests a division or separation within the sphere of divinity itself: the exile not only of the Jewish people, but of the *Shekhina* or milder female aspect of divinity from her sterner male partner. The sadness of separated lovers or of children separated from their parents thus takes on a deeper note of sadness, the sadness of a world divided at its root and groaning for wholeness.

As far as Agnon is concerned, such concepts were familiar to him from his reading in kabbalistic texts—the writings, for instance, of the great hasidic rabbi, Nahman of Bratzlav (1772–1811), to which he was much drawn from his youth and which left a deep imprint on his work.[3] There he would have found as a constant underlying theme the notion of the divisions and tensions in the Creation which require healing. Healing is for Rabbi Nahman the task of the Saints or *Hasidim*; but the remedy is not always easy to find, and we are left with a sense of tragic loss, of a world as yet unredeemed. This is the kind of deeper resonance which is clearly present in the symbolism of *Agunot*. In Agnon's later novels and tales, the symbolic meanings are less patent, less of the surface, but they are there nevertheless, and it has been a major aim of Agnon-criticism to seek out and establish them.

Following *Agunot*, Agnon wrote a longer novella dealing with the theme of the abandoned wife. It was *Vehaya He'Akov LeMishor*, 1912 (*The Crooked Shall Be Made Straight*). This tale is much less fairy-like, much more firmly located in time and place. The place is Buczacz; the time, the mid-nineteenth century. We hear of a well-to-do shopkeeper, Menashe Haim, who suffers repeated setbacks in business until he is forced to leave his childless wife and take to the road to beg a living in the villages and towns of Galicia. It is a picaresque tale with many episodes and digressions—some of them humorous—but there is an overarching theme of bereavement and longing, giving tension and unity to the narration. The highly mannered style of the early chapters gives way to a more direct manner halfway through as Menashe Haim becomes an erring human being individualized by folly, piety, and misfortune.

Menashe's first act of weakness is to sell the letter of recommendation he carries from the rabbi of Buczacz in which he is identified by name, and which calls on all good Jews to succor him. He sells it to a worthless fellow, by profession a beggar like himself. Having thus failed once in his charge, he fails again even more egregiously by taking a turn to the great fair at Leshkovitz (something like Vanity Fair in Bunyan's allegory) instead of going directly home with the money he has collected. There he indulges in the pleasures of the fair including abundant food and liquor, and he is naturally robbed of his money. He is now in no position to go back home. He is not only despoiled in a material sense, but he has also, in a manner, lost his identity along with the letter he has sold. Now he is unknown and unidentified, dogged with misfortune. The worst blow is struck when he finally reaches his hometown years later. There he finds that his wife has remarried and has borne a child to her second husband. She had been released from her *aguna*-status by the town rabbi, for the beggar to whom Menashe had sold the rabbi's letter of recommendation had died and the letter found on him had been sent to Buczacz as a confirmation of the death of Menashe Haim. Now comes the real tale of separation. Menashe cannot reveal his identity for this would be to ruin the life of his wife and her child, and bring scandal and dishonor on them all. He finally discovers the grave in which the falsely-named beggar is buried and on which Krendel Tcherni, his wife, has erected a fine tombstone. It is the tombstone which releases him from total oblivion and restores to him his lost identity, for he tells his story to the sexton who, on his death, transfers the stone from the grave of the false Menashe Haim and places it on the grave of the true Menashe Haim. When Krendel Tcherni visits the grave, her tears now mingle with his dust.

Although a realistic tale of Jewish life in eastern Europe in the nineteenth century, *The Crooked Shall Be Made Straight* clearly has allegorical overtones. It is in this respect not unlike Adelbert von Chamisso's famous novella, *Peter Schlemihl* (1814), by which Agnon may have been influenced. Chamisso's hero sells his shadow (i.e., his identity) to the devil for money, and in the end loses both money and shadow, and becomes (like Menashe Haim) a homeless wanderer. The separation, which the *aguna*-status signifies for Agnon, becomes a symbol for some deeper loss. Menashe Haim and Krendel Tcherni are tragically separated from one another, but more than that, they are separated from their true selves. Their lives have become false and unauthentic, their true names lost. But there is no total alienation. The ending is sentimental, but is nevertheless integral to the novel. Menashe Haim who has never forgotten Krendel—just as she has never forgotten him—will regain his identity in the grave, and with his death she too will be released from her false status. There is a certain somber putting-to-rights in death itself.

The story evokes a grim, Hardy-like vision of hap and mishap, but it does not suggest a world totally without meaning. On the contrary, there is a certain logic in its moral structure. Menashe pays for his sins and weaknesses, and there is just a perceptible hint of salvation at the end. The Crooked is, after all, made Straight, though at an unbearable cost in pain and suffering.

Agnon's success was immediate. Here was a tale of the life of the *shtetl* or small township that was neither naively pious nor violently anticlerical and satiric in the manner of certain earlier writers, such as Judah Lob Gordon or Mendele Mokher Seforim. Here was a writer who did not hide himself from the ugliness and inhuman hardship of Jewish life in eastern Europe, but who could yet write of it with tragic understanding and with a sympathy for the principles which upheld it. In a sense, the whole Agnonic vision of this life is based on the *aguna*-motif. Man is beheld bound by common loyalties and a sense of spiritual purpose, and yet he is somehow alone and lost, a wanderer and an exile, finding salvation only in death.

The same theme is repeated on a grander scale, though with a more cheerful emphasis and a happier ending, in a long novel which Agnon began to write in the 1920s, if not earlier, publishing fragments as he went along. This novel finally appeared in 1931 as *Hakhnasat Kala* (*The Bridal Canopy*)—a great work of nearly five hundred pages. It tells of a pious Jew, Reb Yudel the *Hasid*. The *Hasidim* were a sect who emphasized the religion of the heart, and they flourished among the poorer classes in the east-European Jewish townships from the mid-eighteenth century onward. Reb Yudel the *Hasid*, is blessed with three daughters but is without the means of supporting them, and more particularly without the means to marry them off. He therefore takes to the road in order to find a dowry and bridegrooms for his daughters, and he too, like Menashe Haim before him, is furnished with a letter of recommendation, this one from the great hasidic wonder-working Rabbi of Apta.

Bidding farewell to his pious and gentle wife, Frummit, Reb Yudel goes off to make his family's fortune. It is like *The Crooked Shall Be Made Straight,* redone as comic-epic-fable. Reb Yudel is the Jewish Joseph Andrews, or rather Don Quixote. As innocently free of guile or doubt as Don Quixote, and with a sunny hasidic temperament based on the three cardinal principles of joy, humility, and devotion, he goes confidently on his journey borne on a horse-drawn cart and accompanied by the Sancho Panza-like carter, Neta. The description is marked by a mixture of the fabulous and the absurd, but there is a real landscape too, though Reb Yudel is blithely unaware of it.

And so they kept going toward the southwest amid treeclad forests which hid the occasional robber, and without stopping they passed through the non-Jewish villages of Hutnik and Kuzmir. There the little urchins came out to throw stones at them. "Stick your head into the cart, Reb Yudel, or you'll get hit," cried Neta. "I," said Reb Yudel "have no fear of them, for have I not already pronounced the prayer for wayfarers?" Neta gave the horses a smart lash thinking to himself, the world is mad indeed when his two horses Moscheni and Norutza have to be harassed because of an idiot such as this. But Reb Yudel is away on the wings of lofty meditation. "The great *Hasid*," he said, "has written in his book, 'Duties of the Heart', that man is composed of body and soul joined together, and that both owe their sustenance to the bounty of the Creator. Now that the soul has had its due sustenance in prayer it is sure to watch over the limbs so that nothing can possibly happen to them." Not too long afterward they found themselves in the Jewish village of Pinkiwitz.[4]

The story is mediated through the ironical narrative voice which by no means shares the sanguine piety of Reb Yudel and yet relates to it with warmth and sympathy.

The result of all this is a mixture of innocence and

experience. In the world of joy and holiness, which is the interior world of Reb Yudel, nothing can seemingly happen to him. But the hardship and heartache are there just below the surface. We are constantly reminded by the narrator of Frummit and her daughters sitting at home in dire poverty, trying to earn their bread by plucking feathers from the chickens intended for the tables of their wealthier fellow-Jews of Brod. All this time Reb Yudel moves from one village to the other basking in the sunshine of wisdom and *Torah*, and making little visible progress toward his object. In the end, he will return to his family and marvelously achieve both a dowry and bridegrooms for his daughters. For the moment the harsher laws of this world are suspended, joy and innocence reign supreme. The cockerel which they are taking to the slaughterer flies away and guides Reb Yudel's daughters to a cave where in fairy-tale fashion they find the treasure on which they will all live happily ever after. The story ends in delight and fantasy. But the ironies are not forgotten. The beatific vision of Reb Yudel can exclude for himself, but not for the reader, the world of harder experience. As though to illustrate this, we see him comically at the end awaiting his moment to "go up" to settle in the Holy Land. His eyes we are told are permanently blindfolded so that he should not be able to take pleasure from the sight of anything outside the Holy Land. This may keep away the sight of the stone-throwing urchins from Reb Yudel but it does not keep them away from us, and we remain wryly conscious of how precarious is the basis of Reb Yudel's beatific vision. It cannot altogether annul a world of *agunot*, of abandoned wives and daughters, of hardship and separation.

The Bridal Canopy is structurally a combination

of epic and picaresque. The hero's slow journey through the villages of Galicia at the beginning of the nineteenth century is typically picaresque. With Reb Yudel we encounter mendicants, burghers, students of the law, functionaries of all kinds, the rich and the poor. They provide the material for endless adventure, incident, legend, even dreams and beast fables. What makes it epic is the sense of a universal, or at least a collective, experience. It is not just Reb Yudel's adventures that we witness, but the life of a whole society of "happy fools" like himself, all of them, in a manner, emboldened by the same faith and the same promise. It is one of Agnon's great achievements in this novel that he creates a world of spiritual meaning, and through his compulsive narrative voice makes us accept it and inhabit it. The overall atmosphere of hasidic spirituality involves all the characters, and the reader, too, in its warmth.

It is this wider drama, that of a whole society experiencing the trials of history, which has caused critics to speak of this book and others of Agnon as "epics."[5] Behind the trivial adventures there is a sense of more momentous purpose; there are also—what a picaresque narrative usually lacks—unifying motifs. One of these is the letter which Reb Yudel carries from the great Rabbi of Apta. It suggests responsibility. Its terms[6] are what oblige Reb Yudel to remain in exile, but its terms also guarantee that he will return and be rewarded for his faith. The story of Israel, for all its cruel wanderings, is ultimately a story of hope. Reb Yudel will return to his family at the end, like Homer's hero in the *Odyssey*, and the stream of picaresque incidents will be brought to a conclusion. The separation and pain will be seen to have some kind of meaning in the greater plan of providence both for Reb Yudel and for the collectivity of Israel to whose pilgrimage, through the wilderness of this world, his journey is symbolically related.

An important short novel which has at its center the theme of alienation of souls' partners is *Shne Talmide Hakhamim Shehayu be'Irenu*, 1946 (*Two Scholars who Lived in our Town*). Here the two main characters are not man and wife or father and child, but two students of the Law who should have been bound together by love and mutual respect and, instead, are tragically separated. Reb Shlomo is, as his name Shlomo-*Shalom* implies, mild and peace-loving; his colleague, Reb Moshe Pinehas is (like his biblical namesakes) sharp-tempered and zealous. In addition, he is of a poor, lower-class background as against Reb Shlomo who is wellborn. An unfortunate remark by Reb Shlomo never forgiven by Reb Moshe Pinehas sets in train a lifetime of bitterness between them, causing both rabbis to endure needless suffering, ending only in their deaths. Their families as well as the communities they serve suffer also. Here we have a suggestion of class war between rich and poor, wellborn and undistinguished—divisions which certainly embittered the social life of the Jews in eastern Europe at the period in which the story is set, namely, the mid-nineteenth century. But the symbolic meaning is also clear. Reb Shlomo and Reb Moshe Pinehas represent divisions in the spiritual world. There is a kind of cosmic rift as a result of which love and judgment, righteousness and peace—instead of kissing one another as in Psalm LXXXV, 11—are torn apart, and the two scholars instead of living in harmony with one another become lost souls.

HaRofe Ugerushato, 1941 (*The Doctor's Divorce*) represents the other pole of Agnon's world. Set in central Europe in the thirties, the story tells of a Viennese Jewish doctor and his wife, both of them intelligent, modern, and sophisticated, but in the end they prove to be lost souls no less trapped in the ambiguities of their fate than the characters in the rabbinic and hasidic stories we have considered. The doctor's wife, Dina, is a nurse who shares his interests, and their union is evidently all it should be. But we discover soon that they are both burdened with their past and that this burden will be their undoing. Dina has admitted before their wedding that she had once yielded to another man, a minor official in the legislature. They had parted, and the affair was long over. The doctor, enlightened and scientific as he is, convinces himself that the matter, though odd, has no real significance and he banishes the thought of her previous lover from his mind. But the thought will not be banished; at the ceremony itself and on their wedding night it returns to plague him until finally it grows into an obsession which poisons their relationship. He imagines the fellow everywhere, among the guests at the wedding, in the next room at the hotel; he dreams of him by night and the thought of him remains with him by day. Finally, there is nothing left but to end their distress and be divorced. It is Dina who utters the word divorce first, saying "let us do what is destined for us from on high." And the doctor is bound in the end, sadly and reluctantly, to agree. But just as their marriage was blemished and incomplete, so their divorce is somehow no divorce:

But in my heart, my friend, the smile on her lips remains, and I see that blue-black in her eyes, as on the day I first saw her. Sometimes at night I sit upright in bed like those patients she used to take care of and I stretch out both my hands and call out, "Nurse, nurse, come to me."[7]

This is seemingly a modern psychological study comparable to George Meredith's *Modern Love*. But there is more to it than that. Though the atmosphere is secular with little overt religious symbolism, there can be no doubt that *The Doctor's Divorce* is typologically related to the theme of *agunot* and ultimately to "the exile of the *Shekhina*," and so to the inner core of Agnon's beliefs. Specifically, it may be suggested that this short story of Agnon recalls the account given in *Hosea* of the prophet's relation to his erring wife Gomer. Like the doctor in Agnon's story, Hosea takes Gomer to wife knowing her to have been unfaithful, but her unfaithfulness gives him no rest. Behind all this, is Hosea's real theme—Israel's "affair" with the heathen gods, the *Bealim*. This is the fundamental betrayal. The relevance of this to Agnon's tale is not hard to perceive. He too is describing a society alienated from its traditional loyalties, in danger of losing its identity in a pagan world (the Nazis are mentioned at the beginning of the story) which threatens to close in on it.

Perhaps the parallel with *Hosea* is ultimately ironical and its significance is in what is missing from Agnon's version, viz., the prophet's vision of renewal. The doctor will not bring Dina back and say to her at the end: "I will betroth thee to me forever; and I will betroth thee to me in righteousness, and in judgment, and in love, and in mercy . . . and thou shalt know the Lord." In the less enchanted world of Vienna in the 1930s this happy outcome is improbable. Alienation has bitten deep and is now part of the human condition. It is no longer possible to create a total spiritual environment such as that which we found, for instance, in *The Bridal Canopy*. It is only by an act of spiritual recall that we can evoke the wholeness of such a true love relationship, and ironically we achieve that kind of spiritual intuition only when we are alone and bereft. It is when they have undergone the formalities of divorce that the doctor will turn, in love and longing, to his estranged bride and cry "Come to me."

3

The Childhood Oath

Christian typology is much in fashion nowadays. Literary critics tend to find religious ideas and symbols in texts (such as Chaucer's tales or Shakespeare's comedies) which are often worldly in the extreme and lacking in overt concern with Christian doctrine. In Agnon's case, the typological approach is far more obviously in place, for his concern with the underlying spiritual issues is indicated by numerous hints and by the use of a style heavily loaded with biblical and rabbinic echoes. At the same time, his stories have, as we have seen, a high degree of realism. They are symbolic, but they are also rooted in particular times and places, and often based on the lives of real people. They belong to a category similar to that which Erich Auerbach has defined as *figura*.[1] Auerbach's model is Dante's *Divine Comedy*. The presentation there, for all its weight of symbolic meaning, never relinquishes its hold of real human experience in a this-worldly context.

Agnon's tales and novels are "figural" in this way. There is no denying their further meaning, their emphatic way of pointing beyond themselves, but at the same time there is no denying their concrete historical circumstantiality. The characters in *The Doctor's Divorce* exist in a fully realized milieu, and yet they are a "figure" for more inclusive, more mysterious truths. The one aspect does not contradict the other. They do not cease to be a Viennese doctor and his unhappy wife in the year 1930 when they also seem to personify the ambiguities in the covenant relation between God and Israel.

A second major symbolic motif in Agnon's stories, not unrelated to that of the *aguna*, is the childhood oath. A man and a woman bound to one another through their own promise or through that of their parents or through some predetermined affinity, drift apart or deny one another. But the past will not be mocked; its shadow lies across the present bringing with it madness and unappeasable longing. This theme is not confined to Agnon. At the time that Agnon was writing his early stories, it was being dramatized on the Hebrew stage as the basic plot of S. Anski's *The Dybbuk* (1916). In that play, Lea and Hanan are promised to one another before birth, but Sender, the wealthy father of Lea, has transgressed the oath by giving his daughter to another bridegroom. In the tragic sequel both Lea and Hanan die. The fable had an obsessive interest for Jewish communities in all parts of the world, but most of all for the new settlers in Palestine. They were the heirs of age-old promises and oaths. But they had sought new ways, and the attempt to break free caused them great spiritual conflict. It is this conflict that *The Dybbuk* powerfully dramatized. Only in death was a catharsis possible.[2]

Agnon's most important treatment of this theme is in his hauntingly beautiful *Shevuat Emunim,* 1943 (*Betrothed*). This story tells of Jaffa before the First World War, with its small but colorful community of traders, officials, intellectuals, and the occasional farmer. Dr. Jacob Rechnitz, a young scholar hailing from central Europe, teaches German and Latin in the local high school to the sons and daughters of the settlers. Everything is straightforward and realistic, and we may be sure that Agnon here has drawn heavily on his own observations of the life of the period and of the locality which he knew so well. But there is a remoter, more occult dimension to the story: it is symbolized in the first place by Rechnitz's chosen hobby, that of collecting and classifying the seaweed that he finds on the beach. This interest, first kindled at the university, becomes for him a scientific passion. He is a methodical scientist, a botanist of the sea, whose discoveries are published in the professional journals dealing with this curious specialty. Eventually his labors will be recognized, and he will be offered a professorship in an American university. But if the academic aspect of his profession is stressed, the romantic aspect is not lacking. He can say with T. S. Eliot's Prufrock,

> I have heard the mermaids singing, each to each . . .
> We have lingered in the chambers of the sea
> By sea-girls wreathed with seaweed red and brown.

The sea-girls are seven: six of them are young ladies of Jaffa, Rechnitz's older pupils who are in the habit of promenading with him on the beach talking of poetry and of more mundane things; the seventh and more mysterious maiden is Susan (*Shoshana*), the daughter of the consul Ehrlich from Rechnitz's hometown of Vienna. They have been known to Rechnitz from his earliest youth, and now they have come to Jaffa on a visit after touring many parts of Africa and the east. The oath of undying love which binds Susan and Jacob together was first uttered by them in her father's garden when they were both small children. Susan had once jumped into a pool in that garden and had emerged, we are told, covered with seaweed like a veritable mermaid. At Susan's request, Jacob repeats the childhood oath on the beach at Jaffa amid the sound of the waves, whilst a solitary fisherman stands waist-deep in the water. The two scenes are thus symbolically blended with one another.

It is easy to see to what region of archetypal symbolism the sea, the seaweed, and the mermaids belong. They symbolize the past ages. Jaffa is, after all, reputed to be the oldest port-city in the world. The setting suggests the depths of spiritual memory. The sea-symbolism takes us back to the origins of our life as individuals, as members of a nation, and as members of the human race. It signifies the attachment of Rechnitz and Susan to their common beginnings, and to the oath of eternal love and loyalty that they have sworn:

At the sound of the waves, at the sight of the limitless expanse of sea, Rechnitz closed his eyes. And now he saw his mother kneeling down before him. He was a small boy; she was threading a new tie round his collar, for it was the day Susan was born and he was invited to the Consul's house.[3]

Here the bond linking Jacob and Susan is taken back to the day she was born. It represents the weight of the past, its sweet inexorability. But sweet as the memory of his and Susan's youth is, it is also compounded with images of death (the death of her mother who also in a mysterious way is confused with his own mother), and with a sense of constraint and sadness. Upon Susan lies the shadow of disappointment and of melancholy far-off things. Moreover, she draws Jacob with her into the sphere of her own obsessive rootedness to the past. A supporting motif here, which picks out the connection of Susan with death and the past, is her interest in Egyptian mummies. The eternal life which Egypt gave to her sons is the existence for which Susan yearns, the petrified existence of the mummy. Her words echo the rhythm and imagery of the book of *Job*:

Then forgetting all about the cigarettes, Susan went on, "Our days on earth are like a shadow, and the time of our affliction is the length of our days. How fortunate are those mummies, laid in the ground and freed from all trouble and toil. If I could only be like one of them!"[4]

Her wish is soon granted. She does not die, but she succumbs to a strange and paralyzing ailment, a form of sleeping sickness which serves to deepen the gloom which descends on those who love her—her father and Jacob. The doctors of Jaffa can do nothing for her; and so, day after day, she remains living and not living, suspended in the world of the past. She is in a state of suspended animation, whilst Jacob, having received his invitation to take up a chair in an American university, paradoxically turns back tc his work with recovered energy:

Never in his life had Rechnitz been so free a man as now; he had separated himself from Rachel and Leah, from Asnat, Raya, and the rest, on account of Susan Ehrlich; he had come to despair of Susan because of her disease; his journey lay before him, and yet even this was put out of his thoughts in order that work might be his sole object and end.[5]

His new-found freedom and energy underline for us the fact that while Susan is arrested in the life of the past, Jacob's existence is oriented toward the future. He is a scientist, a new man, starting out on a new and interesting career, speaking the new Hebrew of the new settlers in the new-old land, while Susan still thinks of Hebrew as the language of the prayer book. He looks westward to America, while she looks backward to the encrusted conservatism and ordered gravity of the Austro-Hungarian Empire. But though Jacob might turn away from it, the past is not to be eluded. In the end Susan will rise from her bed in a state of somnambulism, and she will win her beloved by means of a moonlight race along the shore with the other six maidens. Having run her race, she will be crowned with a garland of dried seaweed taken from Rechnitz's desk. Thus she captures Rechnitz for herself and by a superhuman act of self-renewal brings about the fulfillment of their age-old vows. The ending is neither joyful nor sad; it betrays instead the fundamental ambiguity of Agnon's experience of history and tradition:

Suddenly there was a voice calling him by name, a voice that came, as it were, from beneath Susan's eyelashes. Jacob shut his eyes and replied in a whisper, "Susan, are you here?" Susan's eyelashes signaled assent. She put out her hands, took the crown from Jacob's arm and placed it on her head.[6]

It is obvious, even if a host of verbal indications in the Hebrew original did not make this clear, that Jacob is Israel (they are historically identical), and Susan (*Shoshana*—the lily of the valleys in the *Song of Songs*) is the divine partner, or *Shekhina*, representing Israel's religious destiny, the burden of past vows and past responsibilities. In a particular sense, Susan can be identified as the Sabbath day,[7] and this is borne out by the rabbinic interpretation of the "seven maidens" of *Esther* 2:9 from which the motif of Agnon's "seven maidens" is originally drawn. This is another strand of hidden meaning in the story, though on the surface it has nothing to say about the observance of the Sabbath day in Jaffa or anywhere else.

The combination of such symbolism with a matter-of-fact story of a quite different sort may surprise the reader of modern realistic fiction. But this combination is not altogether unknown in modern fiction. After all there is Kafka, and there is Joseph Conrad who wrote sea tales and tales of adventure which nevertheless had inward psychological and symbolic bearings. Agnon, in *Betrothed*, has written the history of Jaffa in the time of the Second Aliyah; he has also written a symbolic fable portraying the bond linking Jacob-Israel and the *Shekhina*—the sleeping beauty of the fairy tale who can be aroused from the sleep of the centuries only by the kiss of her destined spouse.

Ido Ve'Enam, 1950, (*Edo and Enam*), an even more mysterious tale, introduces another sleepwalking heroine, Gemulah, a lady of strang ancestry living in Jerusalem with her husband Gabriel Gamzu. There is a suggestion, however, of two previous bonds: the one, a prenatal promise binding her to a certain Gadi ben Geim, the child of a neighbor in her native country in the far-off mountains of the east; the other, a secret bond with a philologist, Ginath, who had visited her when she was a girl and had learned from her lips the ancient language of Edo. Her destiny is more firmly linked to his because Dr. Ginath has come into the possession of certain inscribed leaves of papyrus preserved from the ancient past. (This detail was probably suggested to Agnon by the discovery at the time of writing this story of a number of very ancient scrolls in a cave near the Dead Sea, and their identification by the archaeologist, Eliezer Sukenik.) These leaves control Gemulah's movements in some extraordinary fashion, so that when she goes out on her sleepwalking expeditions she is drawn as by a magnet to the study where Ginath is working on his ancient languages. Clearly, the ancient documents symbolize something handed down from the "past." As in *Betrothed*, there is the same overarching theme of the past weighing down the present. In fact, Agnon draws the connection and humorously compares the Enamite leaves with "such weeds as Dr. Rechnitz drew up from the seas near Jaffa."[8] Gemulah's language and the language inscribed on the leaves is that of the past, a dead language; but Dr. Ginath, the antiquarian scholar, has the key to it, just as Rechnitz had the symbolic possession of the past in the dried seaweed.

Gemulah belongs completely neither to Ginath nor to Gamzu. Ginath, a cold European-type scholar, views her with scientific detachment. Gamzu, lover of tradition and former Yeshiva student, has an emotional attachment to her but is incapable of understanding her secret life. Ginath and Gamzu thus represent the divided halves of the Jewish people in their ambiguous relation to the past. The outcome of the relation is disaster. In one of her midnight walks, Gemulah is seen climbing onto a roof; Ginath attempts to rescue her but they both fall to their deaths, and Gamzu is left alone, bereft and widowed.

It may be noted here that the childhood oath represents an important strand of meaning. Although Gemulah has come "home" to Jerusalem, she is also held by childhood bonds to her far-off home.[9] The link with Gadi ben Geim underlines the fact that she, partially at least, belongs elsewhere and is thus in exile even in the Jerusalem-setting. Her hope of acquiring a true relation to her new environment rests with Gamzu and Ginath, though neither of them can achieve this for her. But the tale ends not quite hopelessly. The work of Ginath will live on: his books, we are told, are printed in increasing numbers and the world is beginning to know them. The language of Edo and the hymns of Enam, which Gemulah had borne in her soul, will become the possession of a people in the future.

The theme of the childhood oath reappears in a number of Agnon's other writings. Of these, two should be mentioned. A *Simple Tale* (discussed in Chapter 7, pp. 85–96), is a tale of madness and longing which has its genesis in the failure of one Barukh Meir, the father of the hero, to marry Mirel, the girl for whom he had been bespoken. Instead he marries the wealthier Zirel

Klinger. But no good comes of this act of betrayal. From his union with Zirel he begets a son, Hirshel, who will be stricken with insanity, whilst Mirel will give birth to a daughter, Bluma, whose charm and beauty will haunt his son Hirshel and rob him of his peace. Again, a story of longing and unrequited love (between Hirshel and Bluma) having its origin in a pledge made and broken in years gone by. And beyond the longing, the passion, and the sorrow is the sense of a metaphysical wound, a historical fall from grace affecting the life of a whole community.

In Agnon's posthumous novel *Shira,* 1971, the relations between the hero Dr. Manfred Herbst and his wife Henrietta are also based on early memories and pledges. She is the wife of his youth. His estrangement from her and his affair with the nurse Shira carry overtones of betrayal on a wider scale. But here a new aspect is revealed. The longing and the passion belong not to the object of his early love, but to the affair with the "strange" woman. Shira, representing not traditional loyalties and age-old sanctities but rather their opposite, wields a disturbing power over the body and soul of Manfred Herbst. It is a kind of inversion of *A Simple Tale.* Maddened by longing for Shira, Herbst tramps the streets at night searching for a glimpse of her face, looking for her lighted window in much the same way as Hirshel had sought out Bluma's lodgings ceaselessly through the night. If Hirshel's Bluma is the hidden *Shekhina,* and their love reminds us constantly and unmistakably of the *Song of Songs,* here in *Shira* we have, by contrast, the fascination of the unhallowed, the bond not with the past, but with the enchantments of a new world in which past beauty has faded. Shira is not beautiful—this the narrator makes clear—she even has a certain aggressiveness and coarseness in contradistinction to the heroines of the other tales of Agnon we have considered. The bond which ties Herbst to her is thus a kind of witchcraft, an incurable madness lacking grace and beauty. It will profit no one. Agnon is honestly confronting here the fierce attractions of alienation itself, the shadow cast not by the past upon the present, but by the present upon the past. In this novel we glimpse a world which lacks traditional signposts. And perhaps for that reason, this was the one novel which Agnon found himself unable to complete.

4

The Lost Key

It will readily be seen that for Agnon time is a central issue. Our childhood lives with us in the present; past obligations and promises, those of ourselves as individuals and those of the total community to which we belong, remain with us, a presence not to be put by.

Yet, in a different sense the past is irrecoverable. We look yearningly toward it knowing that Henrietta will never again be to Manfred Herbst what she once was, knowing that we shall never again enjoy the patrician charm of the garden and the goldfish pond in the childhood of Susan Ehrlich. Agnon's sense of the past is dialectical; it is eternally present, and yet it is lost to us, as in T. S. Eliot's *The Four Quartets*:

> Footfalls echo in the memory
> Down the passage which we did not take
> Towards the door we never opened
> Into the rose-garden.

Agnon's world has been summed up under the heading of nostalgia and nightmare.[1] When the past is viewed without a living connection with the present, it becomes merely a nostalgic dream, and much of Agnon's writing is nostalgic and elegiac in this way; but when the present is viewed unsupported by meanings derived from the past it becomes a nightmare. When this happens, Agnon's writing takes on a nightmarish quality. Ultimately it is a question of reality. We may imagine that to live simply and naturally in the present moment is to occupy reality. For Agnon, however, the present when detached from the past becomes grotesquely unreal, just as the past when viewed as mere past, i.e., unenduring, fossilized, romanticized, also becomes unreal. What is needed is the purposeful conjunction of the two.

The long novel in which Agnon makes his most

intense exploration of the theme of time—a novel comparable in this respect to Proust's *À la recherche du temps perdu*—is his *Oreah Nata Lalun*, 1939 (*A Guest for the Night*). It has been described as Agnon's central masterpiece, that in which all his potentialities were realized.[2]

The hint for the novel was provided by a visit to his native town of Buczacz in the year 1930. This visit of a few days, after an absence of sixteen years, stirred up in Agnon the memories of the past in much the same way as the taste of the *madeleine* awoke in Proust all those latent memories from which his great novel took its rise. Agnon's narrator therefore is seen to visit his native town of Shebush and to reflect on its past glories and on the experiences of his childhood. There are three time-levels in the novel: there is the time of writing itself, i.e., the middle thirties—the period of the rise of Nazism and of increasing tension between Jews and Arabs in Mandatory Palestine. These matters though not directly discussed cast their shadow over the whole work. Then there is the time of the "return of the native," i.e., the year 1930, which Agnon expands into a full twelve months giving a kind of Greek unity to the work after the manner of Hardy's novel. And finally, there is the time of retrospect, the years of the turn of the century when the narrator was a boy. All the older characters refer back to this period in some way or other. This triple time-scheme creates a complex structure unified by the first-person narrator himself who holds all three together, and shares this multiple awareness with the reader. The effect is to give to the narrator an unusual degree of command over the novel as a whole.[3] He is the main actor, and his is also the consciousness within which the action proceeds, for the important events in this novel are inward events —reflections and memories.

So far, this is very like Proust, but Agnon, unlike Proust, is not primarily recording his private experience or exercising his private sensibility. He is ultimately involved in an epic enterprise, in recording the experience of a total community in a time of change. His theme is the Jew at the crossroads of contemporary Jewish history, before the Wars and between the Wars: one kind of historic Jewish community, viz., the *shtetl*, disintegrating whilst that which was evidently to replace it, viz., the new *Yishuv*—the national community in Palestine—is not yet fully formed and established. All the major characters, as well as having a relation to the past of the *shtetl*, have a relation, whether of hope, disappointment or skepticism, to the new enterprise in the Land of Israel. Past, present, and future are thus beheld in a kind of triangle of forces, with the narrator somewhere at the center of the triangle.

At the opening of the novel, the narrator, a resident of Jerusalem, arrives at the railway station of Shebush on the eve of the Day of Atonement. The first inhabitant whom he sees is the guard on the platform, one Gumowitz, who had lost a hand in the war and has a rubber hand to replace it. The next Jew he encounters, Daniel Bach, is also mutilated. His leg, replaced now by a wooden stump, was lost soon after the war in a train accident whilst he was trying to earn a living by smuggling saccharine into the country. Crippling and loss are evidently the signs of the new era in Shebush. The service in the Great Synagogue on the solemn eve of the fast immediately focuses for us the sharp contrast between past and present. The synagogue seems no longer so "great" as it was to the narrator in his childhood. It has shrunk. It has also become darker; the great candelabra have disappeared—evidently plundered in the war. But these are merely the outward signs of an inner spiritual change. The people in the synagogue are no longer so vitally involved in the meanings of the Day as once they were. Not only have the silver "crowns" disappeared, which once adorned their prayer shawls, but the glory is gone from the prayers themselves. They finish the routine of prayer hastily and shuffle off to their homes.

Walking out toward the river after the service, the narrator, never once identified by name in the course of the novel, meets a group of freethinking youth ostentatiously desecrating the holy day. They have just held a party, and are now smoking their cigarettes to show how little the Day of Atonement means to them. On the following morning the narrator goes to the old *Bet Midrash* (The House of Study) to worship. This had been in times past the true spiritual and intellectual center of the community. He notes how bare the bookshelves now are, and how few people, maybe twenty in all, have come to the service. Most of them do not even possess a prayer shawl. The signs of poverty and decline are all around, and the worshippers tell him that soon after the festival they plan to move out—some to America, others to different parts of the globe. The world of the *shtetl* is becoming empty—emptied of meaning as well as of people. But the past lives with those who are left as it does with the narrator himself. Toward evening at the closing service there is a deeper solemnity, and even the skeptical Daniel Bach, who had earlier expressed doubts as to whether the Day of Atonement could bring either good or evil to anyone, is seen near the door, prayer book in hand, whilst his father, the pious Reb Shlomo, a true and uncorrupted survivor of earlier days, intones the service. The narrator himself has moments of meditation in which past and present fuse together, as for instance when he stands by the window and sees once again the mountainside opposite raised protectively above the *Bet Midrash* as it always had been, reminding him of the time in his youth when he had stood by the same window and had composed his first poems in moments snatched from his *Talmud* studies. In this respect, his visit to the old *Bet Midrash* is like Wordsworth's second visit to Tintern Abbey. It disturbs him with a sense of something far more deeply interfused than he had experienced in the past. And even when walking in the forest, he becomes more intensely aware of its beauty than ever before. "I don't know whether something was added or whether perhaps just my own eyesight had doubled."[4] Paradoxically the visit to his native town thus becomes a new revelation, a way of entering into his deeper self.

This notion of the entry into the deeper layers of consciousness is now strikingly dramatized by an important symbol introduced into the novel at this point. It is the great brass key of the *Bet Midrash* which one of the older inhabitants, Elimelekh Kesar, presents to the narrator scoffingly saying they have no further use for it, and why shouldn't he have it since he seems so drawn to the place where his fathers had worshipped? The narrator takes charge of the key and his emotion is so great that he cannot utter a word. Possessed of the key to the past, he now lets himself into the *Bet Midrash* every day to spend the morning hours in solitary study and meditation, and to find new meaning in old books. But this reunion with the past is short-lived. Arriving one morning at the *Bet Midrash* he finds he has lost the key, and gloom descends on him as he paces round the *Bet Midrash* trying to find a crack or crevice through which to enter:

> But our forefathers built the *Bet Midrash* strongly of stout timbers, doors and locks. You can only get in if you have the key.[5]

Now that the "key" is lost he also loses his zest for conversation with his many friends in the *shtetl*, and he loses his pleasure in his country walks in field and forest. All the world becomes for him a mighty stranger. For after all, it is the past, symbolized by the key, which had given meaning to the present. In this dilemma, Daniel Bach advises him to do as he had done: having lost his true leg, he had made a substitute out of wood. Let the narrator do the same: let him have a new key made to replace the original! A new iron key is therefore ordered, and when it is made and handed to him, the narrator's peace of mind is restored. Once again he can resume his connection with the *Bet Midrash* and all that it represents, but now he does more: he creates a rapport between the *Bet Midrash* and the world around him (the new key symbolizing evidently the possible junction of past and present). Winter is at hand and he brings wood to heat the *Bet Midrash*; he also organizes prayer and study sessions for those who are interested in sharing with him the warmth of the place. A kind of community is established for a short period around and within the *Bet Midrash*.

We follow the key right through the tale. Before he leaves Shebush at the end of his stay, the narrator locks the door of the *Bet Midrash* for the last time and presents the key to a newborn child of some dear friends, at the circumcision ceremony. Significantly, Yeruham, the father of the baby, is not a pious Jew but a freethinker; nevertheless, the newborn child represents continuity and hope. Shebush had long been a place where people died. This birth—the first in some years—and the circumcision that follows it indicate a glimmer of hope. The key is therefore properly handed over to the child by the narrator who acts as godfather.

But this is not the end of the tale of the key. Returning to his Jerusalem home, at the end of the novel, the narrator is astonished when one day his wife produces from his luggage the identical key which he believed he had presented to his godson. Closer inspection reveals that this is not the substitute iron key but the brass original which he thought he had lost, but which had slipped between the folds of his traveling bag during his stay in Shebush and now turned up again in Jerusalem. It is a moment of joy and relief comparable to the discovery by Bunyan's hero of the Key of Promise, enabling him to escape from Doubting Castle and proceed on his pilgrimage to the Celestial City. The narrator wonders whether perhaps he ought to send the key back to Shebush, but decides that the remaining inhabitants would have no use for it, and so he keeps it against the day when, according to rabbinic belief, "the Synagogues and Houses of Study of the Diaspora will find their way to the Land of Israel to be re-erected there."[2] From now on he will guard the key and cherish it:

I entered my house and hid the key in a box, locking the box on the outside. Then I strung the key to the box over my heart. I knew of course that no one was all that interested in the key to our old *Bet Midrash*; but said I to myself, when one day it comes over here to be re-erected in the Land of Israel it is as well that I should have the key ready to hand. Well, the key is tucked away where I put it and I am back at work. But whenever it comes into my mind I say to myself, "The Synagogues and Houses of Study of the Diaspora, etc." Then I open my window and look out to see if they have come trundling back to the Land of Israel to be set up again. But oh dear, no, the Land is silent and desolate, and not the faintest sound of those synagogues and houses of study can be heard. But still the key is safely put away waiting with me for that day. Of course a key made of iron and brass can stand the strain. For me, flesh and blood as I am, it's harder.[6]

The Land of Israel is still not what it ought to be. It remains, in some sense, a desolation. But one day the key will come into its own. The symbolism is clear. The recovered key, which the narrator will preserve against the time when the spiritual treasures represented by the *Bet Midrash* are to be reinstated in the Land of Israel, is the key to the future, just as it had earlier been the key to the past, and just as the substitute key was the key to the present. It is a unifying symbol. More than an isolated motif, it is in a way the theme of the whole novel—its metaphysical depth undiminished by the tone of irony and whimsy with which it is handled.

In *A Guest for the Night,* past and present can still somehow be brought together; the narrator is a sign of that. He finally comes home and brings with him his burden of memories. There is a sense of redemption: the demons of the past have been exorcised, its promises will be in some measure fulfilled. But no such reconciliations are possible in the third of Agnon's longer novels, *Temol Shilshom* (*The Day Before Yesterday*) published in the grimmer context of the year 1945. Although it is set in the early part of the century and refers to events in the period of the Second Aliyah, the overall perspective is that of the Second World War. Holocaust, madness, and death have swept away all recognizable landmarks, and there is evidently no simple key left to the past or the future.

As the title indicates, the problems of time are still uppermost in *The Day Before Yesterday*. We see the hero Yitzhak Kummer making the epic journey from the old-world community of the *shtetl* to the new world of Jaffa and Petah Tikva. From there he moves on to Jerusalem where he attaches himself to the narrowly pious folk of the *Mea Shearim* quarter. But this search for an authentic union of past and present, of innocence and experience, remains frustrated in the universal malaise of his time. The novel is, as we have said, ostensibly located in the first decade of the century, the period of the iconoclastic writer Yosef Haim Brenner who is, in fact, introduced as a character in the novel. Signs of tension and of spiritual disturbance were already visible at this period of the Second Aliyah, and Agnon tends to concentrate on these, from his later disenchanted point of view. *The Day Before Yesterday* is in many ways more descriptively realistic than *A Guest for the Night*. It contains a series of accurate descriptions of people and localities. Moreover, the hero Yitzhak Kummer acts more, and spends less time in mere reflection than the narrator of the earlier novel. This gives the novel a simpler, more straightforward everyday quality. But before long the everyday realism is shattered, and the novel lurches into nightmare to become Agnon's major surrealistic work, with moments reminding one of the more horrifying tales of Edgar Allan Poe. The dog Balak, whom the narrator encounters halfway through the tale roaming the Jerusalem streets, marks the entry of the comic grotesque, and much of the "stream of consciousness" from this point on takes place within the mind of the dog. The symbolism is again transparent. "The face of the generation is like the face of a dog," says the talmudic dictum which Agnon quotes, and in a world fundamentally insane the dog becomes its proper spokesman. Balak represents the dark side of Kummer and, indeed, of the world of the novel.[7] The ending is appropriately nihilistic. In a period of drought, Yitzhak is bitten by Balak who now suffers from rabies. He dies in agony.

Often during the course of the novel, Yitzhak Kummer is contrasted with his ancestor Reb Yudel Hasid (of *The Bridal Canopy*) who had lived in blissful trust awaiting the coming of the Messiah. Yitzhak, who knows the bitter taste of guilt and frustration, is bound closer to reality as we know it than is Reb Yudel. But in another sense, Reb Yudel's world was the saner and truer of the two. It is his kind of faith which had given substance and meaning to Jewish life for many hundreds of years. Has Yitzhak Kummer anything comparable to offer? Ironically we are told that what they both have in common is a burial place in the Land of Israel, the suggestion being, perhaps, that neither idyllic dream nor grotesque nightmare can provide a real basis for the future.

But this is not quite the final conclusion of the novel. True to his biblical models, Agnon delivers his world from death, burning, and madness. After Yitzhak's death there is a symbolic downpour of rain. The problems are not solved, but the parched earth is revived. Man returns to his labor under the sun. After flood and holocaust, we witness the return of fertility as the Land yields its blessing and becomes in very truth, as the narrator terms it, "the Garden of the Lord." Total nihilism is, it seems, impossible.

5

Between Dream and Waking

person narrator, and that his tale is the "key" to the others. If that is so, it is clear that the connecting theme is that of home and homelessness, for the narrator tells us at the beginning that he is using the Greifenbach home as a temporary shelter while they are away because his own house was destroyed in the Arab riots of 1929. Since Agnon's home in Talpiot was wrecked by Arabs in that same year and part of its contents destroyed, his own link with the narrator becomes comprehensible.

Agnon is, like Sterne, a self-conscious narrator. He not only has fun with his digressive-progressive technique but he discusses it with the reader, to the point where it becomes a theme in the novel. Thus, after a long digression in *A Guest for the Night* in which he has been talking to us about a childhood friend Schutzling who, like himself, has come to Shebush for a visit, Agnon concludes whimsically:

So back to our subject.
We have said the same a thousand times before. In the meantime we have forgotten where we were and we don't know what is our subject and what isn't. We started out with the Guest and the Key to the *Bet Midrash* and then we left both Guest and *Bet Midrash* and attended to other matters. Let's hope that tomorrow Schutzling will be on his way and then we'll have a chance to get back to the *Bet Midrash* and enjoy a page of the *Talmud*, and maybe, if it please God, we'll take in the commentaries as well.[1]

Many of the metaphors and symbols in the novels are what we should call reflexive metaphors. They have as much to do with the art of the novel as with the content of the story. Thus the motif of home and homelessness which is so pervasive, for instance, in *Edo and Enam*, becomes a way of defining a technique whereby a meandering tale constantly returns home like the

Greifenbachs who wander abroad and come back home.

Another reflexive metaphor is the "key" of which we have spoken as the central symbol in *A Guest for the Night.*[2] It is a key to the past, but it is also a key to the story that Agnon is telling. If he loses the key it is because he is constantly, as he tells us, in danger of losing the thread of the tale; and if he finds the key at the end, it is because that is precisely the feeling the reader has when the picaresque train of events ends, and the narrator returns to his home in the Land of Israel. The finding of the original key, which the narrator has really had in his possession the whole time, indicates that the true design—the overall epic direction—has never really been lost sight of in spite of the wandering motion of the narration. We can rely on the narrator to bring us home.

We may conclude that Agnon is not as digressive as he seems. Even if we cannot always fathom the connections, we are invariably left with the feeling that there is some kabbalistic undercurrent of significance to give unity to the whole; some key to the seemingly aimless drift of the narration. The characters are by no means free (as they are, for instance, in *Ulysses*) to float away on the undirected stream of their own mental associations. The author is always there either within the narrative or behind it, and he has the "key" to what is happening, even if it is temporarily lost in his traveling bag. To put it another way (using another reflexive metaphor), we could say that though the story may go awry "the crooked is always made straight."

All this suggests that while these stories resemble novels of the "stream of consciousness," there are important differences. There is a more purposive kind of development. This can be illustrated from the kind of reflection or meditation his characters indulge in. In Joyce or Virginia Woolf we are accustomed to what is sometimes called the interior monologue. Characters reflect inwardly, drawing on past experience; it is a relatively unstrenuous form of reflection. In Agnon we have something more dramatic, viz., the interior dialogue. His meditating characters argue back and forth, debating inwardly, using the method of question and answer which the Jewish reader recognizes as the technique of talmudic discussion.[3] Should the Guest have a new coat made?

Now how should I have this overcoat made? And even if I have it made what sort of an appearance shall I make in it? For I am generally ashamed to walk out in new clothes. And why am I ashamed? Is it because I don't want to embarrass the others who don't have new things? Or perhaps because a new coat makes you stand out, and you seem to be clothes and nothing else? Just like that story of the man who went to court the girl. When he came to the girl's father, he was wearing a new suit. Said the father, that shows that his old clothes can't be any good. He won't do for my daughter.

But perhaps the analogy doesn't fit the case in hand and I shouldn't hold off making my coat for that reason. The story is worth remembering just the same. For after all that young man simply wanted to make a nice impression. And what was the result? He was sent off with a flea in his ear, because all they could see of him was his clothes.[4]

Here the interior dialogue touches only lightly on a major concern of the novel, namely the contrast of old and new, and the preference to be given to what is old and good over what is new and merely superficial. Elsewhere, however, it betrays more agonizing problems. Yitzhak Kummer in *The Day Before Yesterday* is torn apart by conflicting standards of behavior. Early in the novel he is tempted by Sonia the girl friend of his comrade Rabinowicz. It is an important turning point in his passage from innocence to experience:

So just where he ought to have been glad he felt unhappy, for his heart rebuked him and told him she belongs to your friend. Said Yitzhak, True, but what am I doing with her? I'm only exchanging words. Ah, but his heart retorted, You are turning her away from him! Yitzhak stood dumbstruck. Who is turning away whom? What, just because I exchange a few words with Sonia, that means I am drawing her away from Rabinowicz? You had better keep away from her, said his heart, so that you two don't get too familiar. Yes, said Yitzhak on reflection, perhaps I ought to get a bit further away from Sonia, but perhaps not all at once.[5]

As the novel proceeds we weigh, through the dialectical probing of these monologues, the distance between the life of *Mea Shearim* and that of the pioneers of the Second Aliyah. The dialogic style is thus the correlative of the inner tensions of the life of the community, the uneasy balance of old and new, of authority and freedom, of movement and inertia.

We may now approach with better understanding another dialectical feature of Agnon's narrative method. I refer to the conjunction of the dreaming and waking consciousness. There is hardly a novel or tale in the vast canon which does not include either a dream or a reference to dreams. Dreams are central to Agnon's understanding of life. Thus at the climax of *The Doctor's Divorce*, the doctor tells his wife of a dream in which her erstwhile lover had visited him and put the blame for the affair on her. It is this dream which proves to them both that their estrangement is past repair. Often, there is no way of telling where dream ends and "real" life begins. The two are contiguous, so that the novels occupy a kind of no-man's-land between dream and waking. Thus at the beginning of *Shira,* the first sight that the hero Herbst has of Shira is one that trails off into dream. He sees a blind beggar moving about among the women in the waiting room of the maternity hospital, and Shira, the nurse, offers him a cigarette and addresses him in Russian. Herbst wonders why she does this since the beggar speaks only Turkish. His surprise becomes greater when presently her limbs extend to embrace the beggar and her body grows larger. But the process soon reverses itself, and she grows smaller and smaller until all that is left of her is her left sandal and both she and the beggar disappear. When he awakes from his brief doze, his wife is leaving him to enter the maternity ward for her lying-in.

The episode undoubtedly symbolizes the strange and inexplicable reversals in Shira's behavior which occur throughout the novel, as well as her lack of inhibition; but more than that, it symbolizes the strange mixture of waking and dreaming, of rational self-possession and irrational compulsion which marks Herbst's behavior. In an important sense, he is throughout the novel like a man in a dream, possessed by forces which operate from below the threshold of consciousness. But he is also fully aware of what he is doing and is entirely critical and undeceived about himself. He is not merely an intelligent man, but is remarkable for his moderation and balance. Herbst is, in fact, both dreamer and judge. This is his distinction.

More often, however, the conjunction of waking

and dreaming consciousness is achieved not in the same character but in twin characters representing these opposite modes of consciousness. Thus in *Edo and Enam*, Gemulah is the dreamer or somnambulist, whilst Dr. Ginath is the wide-awake, wise interpreter of dreams. When she makes her midnight excursions, he is there sitting in his room, pen in hand, ready to jot down the words that she speaks to preserve them for posterity. He is the wise man, the scholar engaged in the study of symbols but never allowing himself to be carried away by them. Whilst Gemulah is lost in the strange world of the hymns of the deities of Enam, Ginath is the analyst, the student of antiquity, for whom the poetry of Gemulah is a subject for scientific comprehension. Whilst she turns to him passionately conjuring him by the mysterious bond which links them, he cooly tells her to go back home to her husband. He does not acknowledge any passional depths. And, yet, for all his rational self-possession, his fate is ultimately bound up with hers. It seems that in order to grasp the reality of existence we need both dream and waking.

In *Betrothed* we have the same dual vision projected into the novel through the main pair of characters. We have Susan, the victim of sleeping sickness, moving and loving in the depths of the dream. Her world is a dreamworld of strange, almost surrealistic, symbols:

That night Susan told Jacob many tales. This was one of them: "Once upon a time there was a king who wished to marry me. This king had a fine palace made of palm fronds, and he also had two wives. One of these wives wore sardine tins in her earlobes to enhance her beauty; the other one looked just like the girl you were walking with on the day I arrived in Jaffa."[6]

Her mind turns to the life-in-death of the Egyptian mummies, and indeed her dreams are of ancient, sad matters. She tells us that she has dreamed of being dead. Her lover Jacob Rechnitz, on the other hand, is ever awake; when he sleeps he does so dreamlessly; he is the scientific student of marine flora, those same flora which symbolically express the profound contents of Susan's entranced memory of ancient things. It is she who (in their childhood) had drawn up the sea-weed from the depths of the pond; it is Jacob who now classifies it. She lives in the past, whilst Jacob lives in the present. It would thus seem to be one purpose of the narrative to bring these into relation with one another.

The digressive and, yet, purposeful and obsessive forward motion of Agnon's fiction has much to do with this conjunction of the dreaming and waking consciousness: the one gives us the symbolic level, the uncontrolled depth and range of association, the radical digressiveness; the other gives us the allegorical level, that ironic, intelligent, and knowing control which the author exercises either from behind or from within the story. In *The Bridal Canopy*, Reb Yudel is himself the dreamer. In Shebush, he dreams of Jerusalem—and this, in a way, is the impulse behind his quest. Sometimes his dream contents are related as a substantive part of the picaresque narration. But, as we have seen, the tone and direction of the novel are not wholly determined by Reb Yudel and his world of symbols; they are also determined by the narrator who tells us of him, and who sees Reb Yudel in a perspective of reality which both interprets and sets limits to his symbolic vision. We share his dream and his messianic expectations, but we also see him as a figure pathetically, even comically, out of touch with a world which denies him his vision.

The thing that should be stressed is that this ambiguity that we are discussing, this mingling of the waking and sleeping vision, is ultimately located in the point of view of the narrator himself, behind whom lurks the author. And it is this ambiguity which determines the story line with its freedom from the ordinary bonds of continuity, and its unabashed use of symbolism in the midst of a real landscape. This is again illustrated in *Edo and Enam.* There the first-person narrator stands outside the orbit of Gemulah's dream consciousness, and is ironically conscious of the irrationalities of the others. And yet, it is the first-person narrator who also gives us access to the world of dreams. It is when he himself is half asleep that he first hears Gemulah singing her strange song, and it is he who reports it to us:

> I am back in my dream again, I thought. The moon shone straight upon my eyes. I said to the moon, "I know you. You are the one, aren't you, whose face was on the picture-postcard." Again, the voice sang, "*Yiddal, yiddal, yiddal, vah, pah, mah.*"[7] The moon lit up the voice, and within the voice was the likeness of a woman.[8]

The ambiguity is thus not only a question of the fictional materials but of the mode of composition itself. It shapes the story line, accounting for its symbolic curve, its circling movement and, at the same time, its determined progress toward a resolution. The author, rather in the manner of a recording in which the singer records his voice twice to produce a harmony, is both dreaming and awake; he is the source of symbolic vision and of moral understanding, the two making up the totality of his narrative voice, as well as the totality of a world which can only make sense as a "waking dream."

Truth to experience is achieved when dream and waking are brought together. It is a precarious balance. In the wild sleep-waking of Gemulah ending disastrously in her death and that of Ginath, we have the violation of the ordinary and everyday, a moment of nightmare; but the ending of the story brings us back to sober wakefulness. We are standing outside the hospital in Jerusalem waiting for the funeral procession to begin, Gamzu is fumbling in his pocket for cigarette paper and tobacco, and there is a policeman to be seen directing the traffic. With the publication of Ginath's papers, as hinted at in the last few lines of the story, the exotic dreamworld of the past will be brought into relation with the ongoing wakeful reality of the present, and a kind of salvation will be bequeathed to the future.

6

The Book of Fables

We have spoken of the combination in Agnon's fiction of the dreaming and waking consciousness, but we have not yet determined what kind of dreams these are. They are surely not typically Freudian or Jungian dreams, though it would be easy to find features to support a Freudian or Jungian analysis. What we seem to have is a specific Agnonian type of dream with a syntax all its own; with anxieties, hopes and terrors which can best be understood against the background of Jewish history both ancient and modern. For this is the fundamental context of all Agnon's thinking and experience.

A work which gives us a special insight into the contours of Agnon's dreamworld, and enables us also to judge its relationship with the world of everyday is a collection named simply *Sefer HaMa'asim* (*Book of Fables*).[1] This is a group of twenty short stories, or rather antistories, written over a period from 1930 to 1951. Here, in these strange writings, the normal bonds of continuity fall away; effects fail to follow causes; the setting of Jerusalem changes without warning to that of Vienna or Buczacz; generations and periods are telescoped. The narrator, for instance, suddenly finds himself conversing with his dead grandfather. Forced to leave his work for a few hours whilst the painters are whitewashing his room, he lurches into the past, into the home of his childhood. The symbolic and everyday worlds are yoked together by violence in a way only found elsewhere in Kafka,[2] though Agnon differs from Kafka in his greater degree of faithfulness both to the dream and to everyday observation. He also reminds us of Edgar Allan Poe with his strange world of mystery and imagination. But, in general, Agnon is not so romantically abstracted from his environment nor so totally immersed as Poe in his own psychic depths. His

Book of Fables are not tales involving radical alienation of that kind.

The last of the *Book of Fables* in the 1951 edition, "The Letter," may be read as a detailed, almost journalistic account of Jerusalem society in the thirties: there are the mandatory police, the bureaucracy, the German refugees with their unhappy complaints about everything they find in the new country. It is all there, even a brilliantly satirical account of a memorial meeting held in honor of some civic leader who has recently passed on. But there is also the faithfulness to the dream. When the narrator gets back home after the meeting, the dead gentleman himself, Mr. Gedalya Klein,[3] is waiting for him; they talk about this and that. There is nothing frightening or unexpected about the meeting: it has all the thoroughly predictable and "normal" quality of a dream encounter. Mr. Klein and the narrator try to find their way to a certain prayerhouse they once visited together (in an earlier dream). Finally, Mr. Klein makes some marks with his stick, and there is the prayerhouse suddenly in front of them! "The old man picked up his stick, knocked twice on the wall, a door opened, and in I went."

A typical dream situation which recurs throughout the *Book of Fables* is sudden amnesia. The narrator finds he cannot remember his address, or that he is tongue-struck, or that his feet are dragging and he cannot move, or that he is improperly clad. In the last case, he is in the synagogue without a head-covering or without a prayer shawl. Above all (as in so many dreams of those of us who have to give lectures or attend meetings), there is an obsession with time. The clock is mentioned in practically every fable: one is inevitably late; the post office is closed before he gets there; he misses the last bus; he has to board a ship by a certain time but the children are lost, and he and his wife chase around the town (which town?) to try and find them, but eventually they get back on board at the last moment as the ship casts off, and find the children waiting there for them.

The three fables I shall describe are "The Last Bus," "The House," and "The Whole Loaf." "The Last Bus" begins with the narrator fumbling with a primus stove needed for boiling water to launder a shirt. Finding there is no kerosene in it, he leaves it and goes off to visit a Mr. Sarit who engages him in conversation regarding various people. The house seems to be a kind of furniture store; it is full of cupboards and chairs, and there is a strong smell of turpentine around. We get a fleeting glance of Mr. Sarit's daughter (by his first wife) "whose green eyes and well-developed limbs put [the narrator] in some confusion." Then Mrs. Sarit (the second) provides him with a kind of launderer's ladle to help him in dealing with the primus problem. Place-names and references to his childhood locate this scene in Buczacz in Galicia. Coming out into the street on a narrow black bridge he finds himself in Jerusalem waiting for the last bus home. A few girls who have been to the theater are waiting at the bus stop, but although they know him they ignore him. One of them has long hair and is wearing slacks. He starts talking to his grandfather but doesn't tell him about his visit to Mr. Sarit, because he remembers that his grandfather wasn't too friendly with Sarit. When the bus comes, he misses it, of course. The girls get in first and he drops the ladle that he is carrying. He is especially exasperated at the thought that the girls have left him behind without even bothering to stop the driver and make him wait for him. His grandfather refuses to let him hire a cab, but takes him to the office of the bus company, where they make inquiries about another "carriage."

I was sorry that my grandfather had lowered his dignity to trouble himself to come from the other world, especially as when he left this one they didn't use buses. I was sorry that I had caused him humiliation.[4]

The superintendent says there is another old carriage but he has no idea when it will start out. The narrator knows very well that it is hopeless to wait for this, but his grandfather urges him on, confident that they will soon move off. The narrator finds his tongue has "thickened" and he can say nothing. The official is obviously having a joke at the expense of them both. On the way to the old carriage (it is really not a bus but, judging by the quaint terminology, it is a disused railway coach from the Galician period) the old man slips and falls, but the narrator doesn't worry because "dead people can't hurt themselves." The problem is what to do now—the narrator starts walking home. It is a pleasant mild evening: he runs into five acquaintances, one of whom he knows by name and who has cause to dislike him. Another passerby of dignified appearance who might have befriended him leaves him with a barely muttered greeting and the faintest hint of a smile. He is left feeling lost and troubled, alone at night "walking behind those men of whom one was my enemy and the other four were not my friends."

Part of the vocabulary of this dream is evidently erotic. There is the ladle, the primus, the girls to whom he is attracted but who seem not to respond to his presence. The sense of emptiness and inadequacy (the empty primus) has evident sexual implications. But this is secondary to the main theme of the various episodes: the young girls just coming from the theater are, as we would say, "moving with the times"—they catch the bus; so is the superintendent who has his laugh at the pair of latecomers who cannot get home; so in a way is Mr. Sarit with his two wives, his successful business, and his careful timekeeping (he goes to bed early and has regular habits). The underlying symbolism of the dream enforces the contrast between the onward pressure of time, and the brooding presence of the past —the grandfather who is "behind the times" and to whom the narrator is still spiritually bound. Hence his inability to respond as he would like to Sarit's daughter and to a girl wearing slacks. His involvement in the "new" world and the anxieties and discomfitures to which it gives rise are a source of "humiliation" to his grandfather. But on the other hand, his involvement in the old world gives him little comfort; his grandfather's foolish solicitude keeps him from "getting home" to his rest, and the patriarchal gentleman whom he meets at the end passes him by with barely a nod leaving him to the company of the somewhat hostile group of Jerusalem residents.

The pervading theme of homelessness is here picked out with clear erotic and historical references. The pressure of onward time, and the remembrance of times past leave the narrator in "great distress." He is an alien in Shebush and an alien in Jerusalem. How will the man carrying the burden of the past and of his own inadequacies and unfulfilled desires finally reach home? The old coach will not enable him to make it, and the new indifferent generation cares little whether he makes it or not.

The historical theme is even more clearly underlined in the symbolism of "The House." We find ourselves in a well-ordered, comfortable and freshly cleaned

Jerusalem house on the day before the Passover. Everything radiates a feeling of domestic sanctity and warmth. But there is also a sense of much activity and tension—the tension arising from the many preparations for the festival. They have not slept the whole week, says the narrator; the house has had to be thoroughly cleaned, the pots changed over, and the last traces of leavened bread have had to be scrupulously removed. There has been haircutting, washing, and baking. The following day, i.e., the eve of the festival itself, will also be a day of intense activity and preparation. And so, worn out with his exertions and in expectation of further exertions still to come, the narrator falls asleep almost before he has a chance to eat his evening meal. His sleep is pleasant and refreshing as befits a man whose home is what it should be on the eve of the Passover, but he is aroused at four o'clock (he hears the clock striking) and, going to the door, is annoyed to find that his nocturnal visitor is "a little Arab boy, somewhat ruddy and stout, of a strain bequeathed to the country by the crusaders." He feels a desire "to strike the little bastard on his jaw" for waking him so rudely in the middle of the night. But he overcomes the impulse and after asking what he wants gives him a drink of water. The child seems to be either impudent or incredibly simple, and remains stupidly where he is. Finally the narrator gives him some of the bread that had been left over before the final clearing out prior to the Passover. This is what the child was after, and he runs away with the bread. Going back to bed he finds he can no longer sleep; he now begins to worry about his landlord who has just got back to town and is threatening him with a notice of eviction. He feels he must go and see him, and try and get the matter smoothed over. In passing, the narrator mentions two customary dreams, one of a pleasant and heart-warming house of prayer in the old country, with its white walls, its candles and its fresh Sabbath smell; the other of a big cold house (evidently in central Europe) of forbidding aspect with many windows and a hostile landlady.

This will help you to understand the feelings of a man like myself, and the fear he has of having to wander, especially of having to leave a place in which I felt at home immediately I entered it.[5]

Looking around for his landlord, Mr. So-and-So, he pursues him from his home to the post office, and then to the bank, but time is short for he has left some leavened cakes at home which have to be finished during the forenoon prior to the festival. He finally meets up with Mr. So-and-So meaning to make some pleasant conversation. However, he finds himself unable to speak. After foolishly following him around for a while, he invites him to his house: to this his landlord brusquely replies that he will visit the house whenever he feels so inclined—indicating clearly that he looks upon the house as his own property and sees the narrator as an unwanted tenant. Finding himself now without money, the narrator has to walk home where, of course, he arrives at a late hour after the festival has already begun. To his profound dismay, he finds the leavened bread left from the night before still unburnt. The table is laid for the festive meal, but all is come to naught—the house is ritually disqualified, and they have to leave it. But the ritual disqualification is but the symbol for a deeper cause of homelessness:

A wife understands her husband. Looking at me she realized that all my efforts with the landlord had been in vain. She knew that we were condemned to leave our home. So she wrapped herself round; she took the boy and I took the girl, and we left.[6]

Going down the street they hear from someone's home the sound of the recital of the Passover Story or *Haggada*, "This day we are here; next year in the Land of Israel. This year we are bondmen; next year we shall be free." Agnon draws the moral:

It is not enough for a man to dwell in the Land of Israel, he must also pray to be free. . . . A home from which you can be ejected at any time is no true home.

This fable cannot be understood without bearing in mind the character of the Passover-archetype, which for the Jew is probably as powerful as any of the Jungian psychic structures. The sense of urgency and haste which the narrator and his family feel is right there in the biblical source:

And the Egyptians were urgent upon the people, that they might send them out of the land in haste; for they said, We be all dead men. And the people took their dough before it was leavened, their kneading troughs being bound up in their clothes upon their shoulders.

(*Exodus* XII, 33–4)

The pressure upon the narrator and his family in the preparations for the Passover is the pressure of the ongoing challenge of Jewish history itself, the Exodus from Egypt being the classical prototype, the concrete symbolization of its terrors and its joys. For the Exodus spells both liberation and exile, and between these two poles Jewish history is lived in all its existential paradox. The narrator has come home: here in Jerusalem was a place where he had felt at home immediately on arrival. At the dream center of the fable it blends with the intimate warmth of the prayerhouse in his father's village in eastern Europe. The first sentences underline the calm and joy which the house radiates from its freshly whitewashed walls, and its sparkling floor. His sleep is the sleep of the man who has come home and presides over the festive board. But it is a troubled sleep. The little Arab boy who disturbs him is descended from some philandering crusader who eight hundred years before had mingled his strain with the local Saracens. He represents that alien series of occupations starting with the Romans—the word "ruddy" (*admoni*) to describe his color immediately suggesting *Edom* the traditional, hated name of Rome—and ending with the British, which has made the Jewish Homeland into a problematical home indeed. Romans, Byzantines, Nabateans, Arabs, Turks, and British have at one time or another taken possession of it, so that although he has come home at last, the Jew has not yet lost the sense of homelessness. He must still fight for his right of possession. The narrator's family ejected from their home and walking out into the street are reenacting the archetypal Passover ritual in terms of modern history.

It will be seen that symbol and allegory combine to form a narrative pattern which gains logical coherence only when the underlying mythic structure is understood. This structure might be termed the Jewish theme of linear history, which though seeming to consist of an endless cycle of exiles and returns, redemptions and catastrophes, is felt nevertheless to be moving on to some desired and all-justifying consummation. Hence the forward pressure, the feeling of having to reach a destination.

The clock is no peripheral symbol in Agnon's dreamworld. In a large number of these tales (as, for instance, at the beginning of *A Guest for the Night*) he projects the experience of the Day of Atonement—another fundamental Jewish archetype—and the constant underlying sensation is that the Day is moving on, it is drawing to a close, there is a further duty still to be performed. Will the narrator successfully discharge the burden of prayer and observance "in the time" remaining? And, always, there is the brooding presence of Days of Atonement gone by in eastern Europe, in central Europe; ancestral echoes and urgent present responsibilities, making together a microcosm of Jewish history.

Joyce in his dream novel, *Finnegans Wake*, celebrates a cyclical theory of history which he had derived from the Italian historiographer, Giambattista Vico. Finnegan blends with Adam, with Tristram, with Sinbad the Sailor and the ancient heroes of Ireland. All the heroes of the past become one hero. There is no change, no progress: it is, in short, an historical pattern which rests upon a nature myth, upon birth, copulation, and death—the pattern of the seasons. Agnon's fiction likewise rests on an underlying concept of history, but instead of the dreamy changelessness of *Finnegan* with its ever-recurring motifs, we have the onward pressure of things to be done invading the inner province of the psyche. Here is the special existential background of Agnon's fiction. The Arab boy has a definite historical existence: he belongs to the present as well as to the past, to the outer world of consciousness as well as to the inner world of the psyche. And the narrator is challenged to react. He will either strike him on the jaw or give him bread. But act he must; he cannot slip away from him into a dreamy indifference. Even in sleep, history throws out to us its challenges and choose we must.

"A Whole Loaf" with the same tendency to the grotesque, and the same obsessive concern with the passage of time as the other two stories just described, is a very much more "contrived" fable. The narrator having been kept indoors during the whole Sabbath day by the intense midsummer heat of Jerusalem, goes out in the evening to look for a restaurant to eat a meal—his first meal of the day. His wife and children are abroad, and he has to manage for himself. Here is a hint of the theme of homelessness we encountered in *Edo and Enam.* An elderly acquaintance, the scholarly Dr. Yekutiel Ne'eman, beckons him in passing and engages him in conversation about his family. They go on to discuss Ne'eman's book, a book about which there is some difference of opinion among scholars. Some say he made it up himself, and some say he drew his opinions from an earlier authority. At all events,

> from the day it was published, the world has changed a little for the better, and a number of people have even made a point of living according to what is written in it.[7]

Before they part, Dr. Ne'eman gives him a bundle of letters which have to be sent off by registered mail, and asks him to be kind enough to take them to the post office.

The narrator, instead of going straight to the post office, turns aside to other concerns. First, he spends some time in a synagogue, then he is tempted to satisfy his hunger first instead of worrying too much about the letters. He walks along daydreaming about all sorts of succulent dishes but makes little progress either in the direction of a restaurant or the post office, until finally he runs into Mr. Gressler who diverts him from both objects. Mr. Gressler is a successful and materialistic hail-fellow-well-met individual, a Mr. Worldly-Wiseman, whom, says the narrator, he had known "as long as I can remember." Mr. Gressler's company had often given him great pleasure, and yet it is also owing to Mr. Gressler that the narrator's house had been burnt down, for it was Gressler who had persuaded a neighbor to set fire to his property in order to claim the insurance, and the fire had spread to the narrator's dwelling. To give a touch of fantasy to the incident it is related that the firemen, who had been at a party when called to deal with the blaze, poured brandy on the fire to keep it going instead of putting it out!

After a brief ride in Gressler's carriage, the narrator jerks at the reins in order to avoid meeting an undesired acquaintance—an inventor of mousetraps—and as a consequence both he and Gressler topple in the dirt, the narrator being badly shaken and bruised. Picking himself up out of the dirt he immediately makes his way to the nearest restaurant, a somewhat classy affair, where he places his order for dinner, adding that he wanted a whole or uncut loaf with it. This would make it a rather special kind of meal. Everyone else is served before him: time and time again the waiter comes along, but it turns out that the loaded tray is always intended for another diner. At one moment he spies a little boy munching a roll of bread,

> just like that which my mother of blessed memory used to bake us for *Purim.* I can still taste it in my mouth. There is nothing in the world I would not have given for just a taste of that roll.[8]

Hour after hour passes until he hears the clock striking ten-thirty. At that he jumps up, suddenly remembering that this is the time the post office closes, and he must rush to mail Dr. Ne'eman's registered letters. Naturally, as he jumps up, he knocks over the tray containing his meal which the waiter is at last bringing to him. The proprietor begs him to wait until a fresh meal can be prepared, and so he waits, full of remorse at having failed in his errand, until at last the restaurant is closed and he is locked in without his having eaten anything. Sitting looking at the soiled tablecloth and the remains of all the meals that have been eaten, he observes a cat and a mouse emerge, both intent on gnawing the leavings. Dr. Gressler passes by the window but fails to respond to his call. At last he falls asleep. In the morning when the staff arrives to clean up, he leaves the restaurant, weary, hungry and alone. The letters are preying on his mind, but it is Sunday, and in the Jerusalem of Mandate times the post office is closed on Sunday.

The symbolism is patent. As Israeli critics have pointed out, Dr. Ne'eman (Faithful) is a *persona* of Moses the Lawgiver, the man who had written a book which some might think his own but which others believe was copied from a greater authority than himself. The world has become a little better since it was written. He lays a charge on the narrator which the narrator must carry out. But the narrator has another friend, the egregious Mr. Gressler. He is the antitype of Ne'eman: coarse, living it up, and caring little who gets hurt in the process. The narrator, though drawn to his company, has in fact little to thank him for. For it is Gressler who, in the past, had brought it about that "his house was burnt down." Here the Jewish historical theme (the burning of the Temple) merges with an event in Agnon's own life, namely, the burning of his home in Germany in 1924, an event to which he often reverts. It is Gressler who diverts him from the task with which Dr. Ne'eman has charged him, and after being diverted, he forgets about the "letters" altogether and concentrates only on satisfying his hunger. This he fails to achieve, partly because in a dream such desires are usually frustrated, and partly because he sets himself a high aim—he wants "a whole loaf," something both satisfying and dignified, something like the Sabbath meal he has missed, a meal which will remind him of the delicious whole rolls which his mother used to bake for the feast of *Purim*. But he is left both hungry and alone. Gressler takes no notice of him at the end of the tale, and amid the garbage and the vermin of the locked restaurant he reaches his nadir. He has satisfied the demands neither of the "id" nor of the "superego." The charge laid on him by Ne'eman remains unfulfilled. But the letters are still in his pocket . . . and some day, maybe, he will get around to mailing them.

Here again we have the Jewish history-consciousness imposing itself on the pattern of the dream-symbols. The clock is moving on, tasks have to be performed, decisions have to be taken. It is not merely that the narrator makes the wrong decisions, but that at the crisis of the story he is unable to decide at all—should he eat or should he go to the post office? This is a natural enough dream-situation. But what gives it its special covenant dimension is the sense of responsibility (the word for "registered" in Agnon's Hebrew also means "responsibility") symbolized by the letters which, though covered with filth, spilt wine, and gravy by the overturned tray, still have to be delivered, together with the sense of a past world not "wholly" recoverable, symbolized by the special meal with its "whole loaf" to adorn and dignify it.

This is clearly an allegorical tale like so many of Kafka's tales, and like *Pilgrim's Progress*; but its force is not entirely owing to allegorical contrivance. We recognize the main features intuitively. We have known Mr. Gressler from infancy, and as for Ne'eman, he has existed from ancient times and he is still around. He reminds us of ancestral responsibilities still waiting to be discharged. Such a tale is thus an image of contemporary existence in the historical present. And here is where Agnon differs from Kafka. "A Whole Loaf" is, among other things, a naturalistic account of a Saturday night in Jerusalem in the twenties. We see the Arabs in their fezzes, the orthodox Jews in their fur hats (*streimels*); there is traffic, there are cafes and hotels; you see the different types coming out to take the air after a burning day of hot desert wind (*hamsin*). You meet the scholar at his lighted window, the successful man of property in his coach; you visit a little synagogue with its candles and benches, and a fine restaurant with its magnificent appointments and its babel of tongues.

If Yekutiel Ne'eman is the Moses of the Bible, he is no less the embodiment of that Moses who still exists as an active part of Agnon's religious consciousness and of the community of Jerusalem which he here describes. Just, as the Arab boy who disturbs the narrator's sleep in "The House" is both a symbol of the red-haired Edom-Esau whom Jacob-Israel had alternately fed and fought in the book of *Genesis,* and a living part of the human landscape of Palestine with which the new Jewish settlers have somehow to reckon. What binds together the world of symbol and the world of everyday is a biblical dimension of ongoing time which communicates with us simultaneously through dream and through our waking consciousness: it is both without and within, both near and far-off, both past and present.

7

A Simple Tale

To regard the surrealistic *Book of Fables* as the norm of Agnon's writings, as some critics have done, can lead to distortion. It is true that this collection illustrates the undoubtedly modern—if not modernistic—aspect of his work. It suggests his break with traditional realism and traditional form. But Agnon's total *oeuvre* is amazingly varied. His bibliography of some two hundred and fifty works of fiction is full of surprises. In many stories he is capable of strict linear progression, and of faithfulness to the unities of time and place. A work which may stand as a superbly successful example of Agnon's adherence to the classical form of the novel is his *Sippur Pashut*, 1935 (*A Simple Tale*). This is a fastidiously controlled work of art, without superfluities and almost without digressions. The author, who remains outside the story (there is no first-person narrator here), pushes straight on in chronological order, remaining faithful through the space of two hundred and twenty closely-printed pages to the life-story of his main character. It is a work which conforms to the Aristotelian pattern. It has a beginning, a middle, and an end, and the behavior of its characters (unlike, for instance, those of *Edo and Enam*) is handled throughout with due attention to psychological credibility.

A Simple Tale, set in Shebush in the early years of the century, relates how one Hirshel Horowitz, the meek and unassertive only child of narrow-minded bourgeois parents, fails, through their contrivance, to marry the girl he loves. She is Bluma, a poor relation, who on the death of her parents had come to work in the Horowitz household. Instead of marrying Bluma he is matched by his mother Zirel with Mina, the only daughter of a wealthy and "suitable" family from the nearby village of Malikrovik. The arranged marriage with Mina does not lead Hirshel to forget Bluma who has, in the meantime, left the Horowitz family and gone to live elsewhere in the town. Bluma, blessed with a tranquil spirit, accepts the situation, but Hirshel after his marriage knows no rest. As he grows in self-knowledge, so his longing for Bluma becomes greater. His marriage with Mina proves to be empty and loveless. We see him tramping around the streets at night in all weathers in search of a glimpse of his beloved. But all that is vouchsafed him is the gleam from her lighted window. Hirshel's unhappiness finally upsets the balance of his mind—there is insanity in the family, and the strain has brought on a mental breakdown in Hirshel. His parents and parents-in-law now thoroughly alarmed, take him off to Lwow (Lemberg) where he spends a period of three months in a sanatorium under the care of an alienist, Dr. Langsam. Langsam's somewhat unconventional treatment is successful. He talks much to his patients but uses few drugs. At the time of the Jewish New Year, Hirshel comes back home, cured. He is reunited with Mina and now we see love slowly springing up between them. No longer does the sad and haunting presence of Bluma come to disturb their relationship. They find physical and emotional fulfillment in one another and in their newborn child. It is indeed a "simple tale," simple almost to the point of banality.

The novel is outstanding for the detailed description of life in the *shtetl* at the turn of the century. We have a minutely observed image of Jewish society in a town of moderate size in eastern Europe. There is, for instance, the new socialist agitation which tends to upset the traditional relationships between housemaids and their mistresses. We see the new Zionist clubhouse where Hirshel frequently resorts to read the newspapers and to talk with his friends; it has taken the place for many of the *Bet Midrash*. We hear of the problems of army service: Hirshel is the son of well-to-do parents of the sort who could generally find a way out for their children by bribing the officials, but his mother uses the threat of army service as an extra reason for expediting the match with Mina—married men being generally exempt. Gedalya Zimlich, the father of Mina, deals in farm products. His expeditions to Shebush are for the sake of buying goods with which to bribe the tax officials in his village. He comes to the Horowitz grocery store (where Hirshel works) to make his purchases. We get a glimpse of the barefooted and hungry Jewish lads from the Russian Pale, deserters from the army of the Czar. Hirshel would occasionally give them an alms. And since this is a story of alliances and misalliances, we learn above all about the local marriage broker, a main part of the social structure. He is Yona Tauber—a sharply-etched portrait, and by no means a standardized satiric one. Tauber, scholar and onetime author, discovered that he had a flair for matchmaking. He never proposes a match directly but, we are told, "no one gets married in Shebush without Tauber having something to do with it." Zirel mentions to him the name of the family and the girl she has in mind: Tauber does the rest.

All the main characters (with the somewhat surprising exception of Bluma who remains distant and mysterious throughout) are fully-rounded portraits, and Agnon has, with the finest brushwork, given us an image of their life and conversation. Here, for instance, is Zirel, telling her husband, Barukh Meir, of her plan for Hirshel. The relationship between the shrewd and calculating Zirel and the weak, ineffective Meir is brilliantly rendered. The narrator remains silent, allowing the ironies to reveal themselves through the dialogue: Zirel has just asked Barukh Meir what he thinks of Gedalya Zimlich's daughter as a possible match for Hirshel. Barukh Meir takes a long time answering. Finally he says:

> We ought to hear Tauber's opinion first.
>
> Said Zirel, Heaven forbid that I should try to take away Tauber's living, but I just thought I would like to know first what you thought.
>
> Zimlich is well-off, said Barukh Meir. There's no doubt about that.
>
> But what of Mina his daughter? said Zirel.
>
> Ah yes, said Barukh Meir, Mina his daughter is a fine girl. There's no doubt about that. But . . .
>
> But what? asked Zirel.
>
> Just that in a matter of this kind you don't really need me, said Barukh Meir. I think you can form a better judgment than I can.
>
> Well I think as you do, Barukh Meir, said Zirel.
>
> So, what do we do? asked Barukh Meir.
>
> Well, we shall have to speak to Tauber, said Zirel.
>
> Yes, just what I said, Barukh Meir rejoined.
>
> You said well, Barukh Meir. That is why I wanted to hear your opinion first, said Zirel.
>
> My opinion is the same as yours, Zirel, said Barukh Meir.
>
> On everything you need to hear other people's opinions, said Zirel. It's the only way to do things. You ask a friend's advice and then between the two of you things somehow get clearer. But so you shouldn't think I do anything behind your back, I want you to know that I have seen Tauber already and spoken to him.
>
> Well, what did he say? asked Barukh Meir.
>
> Don't you know Tauber? said Zirel.
>
> Still I would like to know what he said.
>
> Well, said Zirel, he said nothing and walked off.

Barukh Meir rubbed his hands together with satisfaction.

So Tauber said nothing, eh?

And he walked off, said Zirel.

And where, said Barukh Meir, did Tauber go?

I don't watch Tauber's movements, said Zirel, but I hear he was in Malikrovik.

And what did he do there, said Barukh Meir. Did he keep quiet as usual?

That we shall ask him when he comes to collect his brokerage fee, said Zirel.

Yes, that we shall, said Barukh Meir, rubbing his hands together.[1]

The central and most precise character study is that of Hirshel himself. He is of course the classic *shlemiel*, the best example of the type perhaps in all modern literature. Never acting but always acted upon by others, especially by his mother, he is a pathetic figure but one who somehow preserves the human image. Though he is always pushed around, he makes us aware that those who do the pushing are inferior to him. As a matter of fact, the name Hirshel, through its association with the traditional fool and jester of Jewish folklore, Hershele Ostropolier, is the perfect name for the *shlemiel*. Hirshel is, in essence, a fool. Though he thinks of Bluma all the time, when he finally finds himself alone with her he does not know what to say. He is unable to take the initiative. And even when his tongue is loosened, he remains the *shlemiel*. Later on, for example, he finds himself by his mother's contrivance talking to Mina at a Chanukka party. He has no intention of proposing to her, but his friends seeing them in close conversation begin to make fun of them and to refer to them as lovebirds. Hirshel is embarrassed and, more than that, is deeply concerned for Mina's embarrassment. He seizes her hand in order to apologize, and the gesture is taken by the others as a confirmation that they are betrothed. From that moment on, there is no going back. It is a perfect *shlemiel*-episode.

The *shlemiel* character had been developed in Yiddish fiction long before Agnon came to write *A Simple Tale*.[2] He is the central personality in the writings of the Yiddish author, Sholom Aleikhem, and earlier of Mendele Mokher Seforim. But the *shlemiels* of these writers are fundamentally humorous characters. In Agnon the serious *shlemiel* comes into his own. In this respect, Agnon belongs to the world of Bellow rather than that of Mendele.[3] In the deepening crisis of the twentieth century, the *shlemiel* becomes an image of the human condition—a tragi-comic figure. His significance for the Jewish writer is that, ineffective though he may be in every practical sense, he preserves a certain inner integrity in a disintegrating world. He is therefore a kind of hero, representing, as one student has said, "the triumph of identity despite the failure of circumstance."[4]

The character of Hirshel thus forces us to recognize that *A Simple Tale* is not so simple after all. In spite of its seeming adherence to a realistic formula, and its concern with ordinary middle-class folk, the novel has as much symbolic depth as the other works of Agnon we have considered. The typology is more oblique and the narrator deliberately refrains from pointing out the symbolism, but there can be no doubt that through the character of the *shlemiel*-hero Agnon is here, once again, exploring the meaning of contemporary Jewish existence in a hostile world. It is not simply that Hirshel is a *shlemiel* but that he is the Jew as *Shlemiel*. Ever since the patriarch Jacob was told what to do by his mother and was pushed around by his father-in-law, the Jew has had the sort of troubles that Hirshel Horowitz encounters. But though a victim, he has finally succeeded like Hirshel in affirming his own inner strength, growing inwardly in order to overcome both his own weaknesses and his hard fate. Hirshel is a symbol for the Jew in history. His problem is to survive, to retain his sanity, and somehow to preserve his line for posterity. It may not be very manly to run away from the army of the Czar, but the fact is that the Hirshels of history have more important battles to fight.

Nor are the more mysterious aspects of Jewish existence ignored. They are hinted at by a revealing catchphrase which occurs repeatedly in the novel. Agnon's novels often have such a catchphrase giving its special flavor to the whole work. Here is the phrase: "God in heaven knows." God in heaven knows what is in Bluma's mind; God in heaven knows why Hirshel seeks after her with such unswerving devotion; God in heaven knows how weary Mina is after the uproar and dancing of the wedding feast; and God in heaven knows how their union eventually becomes a true union. After concluding the tale of Hirshel and Mina, Agnon ends the novel with the words:

> We are not yet done with Bluma. . . . Much ink will be spilled and many quills broken when I come to write her tale.
>
> God in heaven knows when that will be.[5]

The seemingly artless phrase through repetition takes on an unmistakable theological load. This becomes explicit in the paragraph describing Hirshel's first sight of his firstborn after returning from the sanatorium in Lemberg:

Yesterday he had said to himself, I suppose as a father I shall have to put up with him now that he has come into the world, but today it seemed to him that he himself had only come into the world for the sake of his son. God in heaven sits on high and plays games with us. He has plenty to do up there, what with building worlds and then knocking them down again, breaking things up and then rebuilding them, and yet he can manage to put his mind even to a little grocer in his shop or to a babe in the cradle. Not that Hirshel hadn't plenty to do—he had; and yet he too could manage to give his mind to that babe.[6]

Hirshel's life is thus a story in the mind of God, a game that the Lord of History plays with a little grocer and his family. Their fate is meaningful because God is not too busy to take an interest in them. And the reason is that they are, in a way, the subject matter of history. History is the record of Hirshel and his like.

Giving depth and meaning to the tale of Hirshel, Bluma, and Mina is, again, the constant symbolism of the *Song of Songs*. Bluma in the Horowitz home blossoms, we are told, like "the lily of the valleys." Her name is the Yiddish for a "flower." And she is specifically the *hortus inclusus*, the closed garden of *Songs of Songs* 4:12. That is why she is mysterious and unattainable. Her name in Hebrew also suggests "closed off" or "sealed." Bearing out this suggestion is the repeated motive of the closed or locked door in this novel. Returning home after Hirshel's betrothal, he and his parents find the housedoor locked on the inside. It takes some time for them to arouse the housemaid who finally lets them in. Later, at the climax of misery and heartbreak, Hirshel is seen trying the closed door of Bluma's lodging as he stands outside in the rain. But there is no entry. "So he laid his head on the handles of the lock and wept." The phrase "*Al Kappot*

Haman'ul" ("the handles of the lock") which gives its title to the volume of which *A Simple Tale* is a part, is from *Song of Songs* 5:5. There, it is the *Shulammite* who puts her hand on the "handles of the lock." When she finally opens the door her lover is gone and she seeks him hopelessly in the streets. Here, Hirshel acts the part of the *Shulammite,* whilst Bluma is the divine lover, now transformed into an unattainable female *Shekhina.* The *Shulammite* we should remember is, in the traditional Jewish interpretation, the personification of the people of Israel.[7]

In the hopeless wanderings of Hirshel through the streets we have a kind of allegory for the historical pilgrimage of the House of Israel. It is not surprising that his sad yearning toward Bluma's lighted window is specifically compared, in the narrative, with the emotions felt on the eve of the Ninth of Av, the anniversary of the destruction of the Temple. It is also no accident that the street to which Hirshel is nightly drawn, in all weathers, in his yearning for some sight of Bluma at her lighted window, is called "Synagogue Street." There is no synagogue there now, we are told, but according to tradition a synagogue which once stood there had been destroyed in the pogroms of 1648. In its place there now stands a church,

> but one wall older than the rest is thought to be a relic of the original synagogue. It is bent over as though in grief, and on the Ninth of Av it weeps like the Western Wall of the Temple.[8]

The symbolic cross-references are patent. Hirshel's love for Bluma is clearly the age-old, sad and hopeless love of Israel for that divine presence which once dwelt in the Temple whose destruction is mourned on the Ninth of Av. The burnt-out synagogue is a Temple-symbol, and Bluma looking through her window is that far-off divine splendor, the memory of which, through madness and exile, Israel has cherished through the ages.

In the light of this symbolism, *A Simple Tale* takes on a new dimension. Dr. Langsam, the alienist of Lemberg, is a curer of souls. His cure consists in reminiscing with his patients about the life of simple piety in the Jewish villages of eastern Europe. The Temple is gone, and the life of exile has dreadfully distorted and degraded the spirit of the Jew (there are few portraits of Jewish family life in Agnon more unsympathetic than that of the Horowitz home), but through devotion and long-suffering (Langsam's name —German for "slow"—is patently allegorical) the Jew can nourish his soul and strengthen himself for his ongoing journey. Hirshel's stay with Langsam corresponds with Christian's visit to the Interpreter's House in *Pilgrim's Progress*. Under Langsam's slow and wise care, Hirshel learns to reconstruct his life. Bluma becomes a faint memory, and Mina becomes for him the object of a real and adequate passion.

It will thus be seen that *A Simple Tale* retains, in spite of its apparently straightforward story line, the multi-layered quality of Agnon's major fiction. Simple and realistically-developed situations reveal typological connections as the story proceeds. Moreover, the digressive mode is felt as something held in reserve. The tales which Dr. Langsam tells Hirshel in the sanatorium are not fully developed, but the mere hints beckon us toward the epic vision. We have a glimpse of a rabbi in a little Polish town dissecting a chicken liver with his penknife in order to be able to assure a poor family that it was ritually fit to be eaten, but the rabbi himself was so poor that he could not afford

In the four years following his death in 1970, three further volumes of Agnon's writings have appeared, and more are promised by his publisher. In fact, the bulk of his posthumous *oeuvre* is likely to equal the eight volumes of Collected Works published in his lifetime. The sheer quantity of invention is staggering. In this concluding chapter, I should like to dwell briefly on Agnon's long posthumous novel, *Shira*, published in 1971 after the three books and the fragmentary fourth book had been pieced together and edited by his daughter Emuna Yaron. It was known that the novel existed and, indeed, substantial portions of the first two books had appeared in installments between 1949 and 1955, whilst the first fifteen pages of Book Three had appeared in the daily newspaper *Haaretz* in 1966. Nevertheless, the publication of the complete manuscript caused widespread astonishment. Here it seemed was something different from all that had gone before. In the account of the irresistible attraction of Shira for Manfred Herbst, Agnon displays the force of physical love with a frankness never encountered elsewhere in his fiction. This is no delicate enchantment of the soul but the power of the flesh, of Eros itself. Shira, vulgar, outspoken and aggressive, is the White Goddess;[1] she is Aphrodite or perhaps more correctly, Demeter, primeval principle of Love and Death. She is neither young nor beautiful, but we can say of her as Shakespeare says of Cleopatra,

> Age cannot wither her, nor custom stale
> Her infinite variety.

But not only did the central personality of Shira occasion surprise, the fundamentally secular atmosphere of the novel came as a shock to many readers. Here was a world as far removed as might be from the pieties of

The Bridal Canopy or of *A Guest for the Night.* It lacked even the balance of old and new that we encounter in *The Day Before Yesterday.*

In *Shira* we have an account of the academic community of Jerusalem in the late 1930s. The men we meet are, on the whole, German-trained scholars alienated from the faith and practice of their fathers. Nor are the family of Manfred and Henrietta Herbst any exception. One of their daughters, Tamara, mingles freely with British officers as well as with her male companions of the Jewish underground. Herbst is neither a believer nor a heretic. He had never rebeled against traditional Judaism for it had hardly received any expression in his upbringing or in his schooling in Germany. Later on he is drawn to Zionism and is helped to a knowledge of modern Hebrew literature by a young medical student from Lithuania who had been trained earlier as a rabbi. But the student dies and disappears from the tale. Nor do Manfred's researches into the civilization of ancient Byzantium awaken in him any spiritual or religious longings. He remains, like the majority of his colleagues, an intellectually assimilated Jew committed only to the sacredness of science and scholarship.

We have of course met this type before in Ginath (*Edo and Enam*), just as we have encountered a secular dejudaized world in *The Doctor's Divorce.* But *The Doctor's Divorce* is short and relatively atypical, whilst *Shira* is a massive epic account of a society unbound by Jewish traditional norms of faith or practice. And although the novel takes place in Jerusalem, a city which could always claim to house a significant proportion of observant Jews, they receive little attention. The pious community of *Mea Shearim* are only mentioned when they are savagely aspersed by Shira in a tirade against the *adukim* or orthodox fanatics.

A more thoughtful reading of the book, however, makes it clear that it represents no complete break with the world of Agnon's major fiction. It provides a new angle and a new emphasis, but the essential landmarks are there as well as the underlying symbolic structure. Shira, it is true, occupies the center of attention, but competing against her is another female figure of a different kind who exercises a milder fascination for Herbst, appearing in his dreams as well as in his waking thoughts. She is Elizabeth Ney, beautiful niece of a scholar whom Manfred reveres, Professor Alfred Ney. Elizabeth is unattainable, not only because Herbst is married and many years her senior, but because she represents a purer virtue than his, that of the *Torah* and the commandments.

Like everyone else in the novel, Elizabeth—a German refugee—is a victim of the troubled times of the thirties, but she preserves a tranquillity of spirit and a calm self-possession which stand as a kind of beacon. Similarly her uncle, unlike the pedants we meet elsewhere in the book, is the ideal man of learning. As Manfred reads Ney's latest monograph, his eyes fill with tears at the display of graceful and authentic scholarship. But Manfred's eyes also fill with tears at the sight of Alfred Ney at prayer at the Western Wall in Jerusalem. And there is a connection between these two aspects of Ney's personality; the narrator tells us what the connection is:

And now I will step outside my role as narrator to tell you something of my own. How did it come about that Professor Ney's researches were so faithful and so accurate? It was because he was the offspring of pious and godfearing ancestors who were accurate in the fulfillment of the commandments and faithful to their Creator. And because they learned to be meticulous in the performance of their duty, so they were meticulous in all their ways. Professor Ney kept their standards and was able to benefit from their merits.[2]

In passages like this, Agnon provides a counterpoint to the prevailing secular mood of the novel. But this counterpoint is not due solely to the presence of Ney who is a peripheral figure; it is not even due to Elizabeth who cannot match the power of the earth-goddess, Shira. It is due to the narrator whose voice provides the non-secular point of view. In the above passage he amusingly announces that he is about to step outside the story in order to express his ideas. He does not always make his strategy as apparent as this, but even without declaring his intention, the narrator, in fact, introduces himself on almost every page. And his is always the voice of the Jew who stands within the tradition. More than that, he speaks familiarly to the reader as one who understands and shares with him his world of discourse.

The narrator thus communicates with us simultaneously on two levels. On the one level, he is closely identified with Herbst—another *shlemiel* figure like Hirshel Horowitz—whose concerns he deeply shares and for whose plight he grieves. And perhaps through Herbst he is also exploring some of his own dilemmas as an artist.[3] On the other level, he addresses us, as it were, on another wavelength. The narrator here is a kind of Gamzu, an ex-Yeshiva student for whom every event evokes a saying of the rabbis or an anecdote about the *Hasidim.* The narrator describes the Sabbath calm in Jerusalem as Manfred walks out one Saturday to visit Elizabeth Ney. For six days men labor and weary themselves, but on the seventh the spirit is nourished with what it receives from the study of the Divine Word. "But," he adds, "these matters did not belong at all to the thoughts of Doctor Herbst. . . for Doctor Herbst was a man of science and his thoughts were about the subject he professed."[4] There is thus a tonal difference between the object of the narration and the world of the narrator, the one sophisticated and alien, the other familiar and traditional.

This tonal difference may be expressed in another way. The basic assumptions of the people described in the novel, the members of the academic community, most of them recent immigrants from Europe, are universalistic. They aspire to belong to the great international world of scholarship. Their concern is with Theodora, wife of the Emperor Justinian, with Greek tragedy and with Nietzsche. (Herbst long toys with the idea of writing a Greek tragedy on the subject of Byzantium.) Greece, Italy, Byzantium, and, above all, Germany are the *foci* of interest for the scholars of Jerusalem. It should be noted that these concerns belong to a world which is not only non-Jewish but even in a large measure sinister, alien and anti-semitic. The reign of Justinian which is the subject of Herbst's researches was also, as it happens, a period of vicious anti-semitic legislation; it has much in common with the modern world of Hitler. In devoting themselves to these fields of pure historical research, the scholars whom Agnon describes are performing a considerable feat of what might be termed cultural self-transcendence, or better perhaps—considering this is 1936—cultural self-immolation. Politically, many of Herbst's friends are liberals and pacifists. The narrator, by contrast, takes his stand on the narrower, more "parochial" ground of Jewish history, both ancient and modern. He is also, as he makes clear, a believer in active Jewish self-defense and a critic of the "Peace League," the do-gooders and the universalists.[5]

Thus we are made to feel ultimately, through the narrator's oblique angle of narration, that with all their impressive achievements, the way of the professors is ultimately misplaced and absurd. One of their number has the expressive name of Weltfremd. It is an absurdity for Herbst to be devoting himself to the burial customs of ancient Byzantium amid the Arab-Jewish troubles of 1936, the gunfire and the curfews. It is a kind of flight from reality. But Agnon drags them back to reality by placing them squarely in the Jerusalem scene of the troubled thirties. From this they cannot escape. Herbst and his colleagues may pursue their phantasms of learning, but they are existentially involved, whether they like it or not, in the dilemmas of Jewish history. This is their destiny, no less than it is that of Reb Yudel, Yitzhak Kummer, or the narrator of *A Guest for the Night*.

This novel has, like the rest of Agnon's fiction, typological hints which enable us to perceive its characters as acting their part—unwillingly it is true—in a covenant-drama over which the God of Israel continues to preside. But it is an inverted drama. No longer is there a simple divine action. The dark side of providence—what the kabbalists called the *sitra ahra*—is temporarily in control of things. In *A Simple Tale* we found Agnon repeating the phrase "God in heaven knows . . ." and thus building up a sense of a mysterious working of providence as it brought light out of darkness. Here in *Shira*, the catchphrase is: "That one who was only created for our harassment." As the years went by, we are told that Henrietta, Manfred's wife, aged more quickly than Manfred owing to the troubles of her family in Germany. It was then that "he who was only created for our harassment" began to trouble him with thoughts about younger women. The Nazis in Germany who murder and destroy, the British in Palestine who prevent the realization of Jewish hopes, and the Arabs whose ominous presence is a constant danger to the Herbst home and garden in Talpiot (Agnon's home in the same neighborhood was wrecked by Arabs in 1929) are all part of the action of that one who was created only for our harassment. Herbst is not really aware of this, and so is bewildered by what is happening around him and within him, but the narrator provides the theological hints. The fact is that, as in *Job,* God has given Satan a free hand to cause trouble. In one episode, Herbst is walking along being irritated by the conversation of a certain Shecherson, a Jewish-Christian, and a bore. Then, as though that is not harassment enough, they are both waylaid and shot at by an Arab armed with a pistol. They are lucky to escape with their lives. There is an evil and restless spirit abroad in the world. It does not let one get on quietly with one's work. If it is not trouble in the home, it is trouble in the streets; or else it is trouble in one's own breast, the trouble caused by obsessive thoughts of Shira, that one who, above all others, was born only for our harassment.

The cumulative effect of these multiple harassments is to suggest that the entire world surveyed by the novel is in some measure off-course. The notion of a diabolical intrusion is also hinted at by the appearance of an important symbol, that of the leather amulet from the township of Ashkelon which has come into the hands of Professor Wechsler. Some thought the strange letters on it stood for the word "Satan" and that it was used in ancient times for conjuring the Devil; others thought the letters were part of a lost proto-Sinaitic alphabet; others thought they were Greek, whereas Wechsler swept all away with his theory that the letters written on it were part of a strange Hebrew word found only once in *First Isaiah,* and which had hitherto baffled all biblical scholars. Agnon is having fun here at the expense of the pedants of the University in Jerusalem. In another chapter of *Shira,* which he suppressed before his death (but which was published separately in 1972 in *Haaretz*[6]), he is even more harshly satirical about the pedants. But what stands out is the link between meaningless archaeological speculations and the theme of diabolical conjuration. The world is out of joint, and the scholars who are traditionally supposed to be men of the spirit, are not doing much to restore harmony. When you move close to them, you will see that they are not only as harassed as everyone else but that they constantly harass one another with their petty jealousies, their vanities, and their ambitions.

Agnon never completed *Shira.* He drafted one ending which would have had Herbst follow Shira into a leper colony, there to cut himself off from the world and devote himself to her till death should them part. But he seems to have rejected this in favor of the fourth book which we have, though in fragmentary form. In the last pages Herbst discovers a new document (of its nature we are told nothing), the effect of which is to stultify most of his researches into the civilization of Byzantium. Now that his work is shown to have been based on false premises, he acknowledges his error and refuses an offer to publish a collection of his articles:

But perhaps the truth newly discovered is itself only temporary and when new discoveries are made these truths too will be abandoned. But one truth remains for ever, and that is the search for truth.[7]

Some kernel of verity is left when all the absurdities of scholarship melt away. Jerusalem is now under siege as the Arab troubles increase. Shira has disappeared altogether, no one knows where. But Herbst remains to the end of the tale—a Jew, still harassed, but surviving in his search for truth. And he will go on, it seems, even after Byzantium and what it stands for has proved a dream, and has faded away into the world of dreams.

Agnon is by any yardstick a major figure in modern literature. He deals with the central dilemmas of twentieth-century man—his alienation from the past and his yearning for sanity and wholeness. His artistic problem, which is that of all great contemporary artists, is to render a disintegrating world in aesthetically balanced form. For Agnon, things are easier in one way because he is the heir of a tradition which is fundamentally committed to salvation even while it accommodates such radical terms as Exile and Holocaust. But things are also more difficult for him than for other major modern writers who have rendered our twentieth-century experience because the symbolic structures he uses, indeed the very language on which his imaginative vision hinges, are the possession of a relatively small culture-group. True, that group rightly claims a place at the center of the history of western man, but the terms by which it translates its singularities into patterns of universal meaning are by no means self-evident. There is also a manifest difficulty in actually rendering his work into other languages. The English translations of Agnon, for instance, are of uneven quality.

Agnon's influence beyond the Jewish and Israeli world is likely to come slowly, for this reason, but in Israel he has been a major force in shaping the novel and short story for a whole generation of younger writers. These men for the most part do not share his religious terms of reference or his unquestioning sense of Jewish identity. They betray very often a spiritual uneasiness which is more like that of the iconoclastic writer of the Second Aliyah, Y. H. Brenner. But Agnon has had the greater "literary" influence. He has liberated many of the younger writers from the narrow modes of social realism that dominated so much of the literature of western and eastern Europe in the early part of the century. He found for them a key which made it possible for them to relate directly to the here and now—the scene of urban or village life in Israel, for instance—and at the same time to apprehend more inclusive truths by means of symbolism. David Shachar, A. B. Yehoshua, and Amos Oz have taken a deep imprint from the dreamworld of Agnon. His *Book of Fables* has become for these and other writers an exciting contemporary model. They are less responsive to *A Simple Tale* with its slower movement and its more muted symbolism.

The real question is: what do they inherit of the content of Agnon's symbolism, its ideological freight? Do they testify to the same world of meaning? Here it should be said that whilst the younger writers often seem concerned with the human condition as a whole, and are less "hung-up" with Jewish issues, they are nevertheless drawn like Agnon to biblical echo-structures and they betray, like him, an obsessive concern with the past. Though they may react against the singularity of Jewish history, they cannot really escape it, especially contemporary Jewish history. Agnon's influence in this respect has been more than merely technical. It is not the craft of fiction, but the meaning of existence that he has very often communicated.

In one story, A. B. Yehoshua speaks of two writers, a father and a son. The older writer is silent, the younger writer is fumbling for speech. The underlying concern is with a past which is no longer an active source of creativity but which continues to dominate the present. Another story (influenced in equal measure by Agnon and Kafka) tells of the keeper of an island prison which is threatened for the fourth time in history by flood and destruction. The sole desire of the keeper throughout the crisis is to remain faithful to the "Manual of Regulations" governing the conduct of the prison, a book emanating from the remotest antiquity, and "divided into chapters and verses, instruction, laws and commandments."[8] The symbolism is transparent. Yehoshua's characters (like those in Agnon's *Book of Fables*) are burdened by seemingly absurd but altogether inexorable responsibilities—responsibility for a prison, for a forest, for a child, for the past, for the future. And along with this sense of urgent responsibility is a sense of immense human inadequacy. These are statements about contemporary man, but more specifically they are statements about the contemporary Jew.

Agnon has not only provided a fictional model for many of Israel's younger writers, he has opened a door into their deeper selves, enabling them to discover and reveal their true identity. Even as they fumble in the dark they can lay their hands on a key. It may not be the key to the old *Bet Midrash*, but it may very well be the key to the key to the key.

Notes

Quotations from Agnon, translated by the present author, are from the standard edition of Agnon's Collected Works [Hebrew], 8 volumes, published by Schocken, Tel-Aviv, 1953–1962.

1. *Introduction*

1. *Works*, vol. IV, chap. 7, p. 30.
2. See *Ezekiel*, chap. 39.
3. *The Rise of the Novel* (Berkeley and Los Angeles: University of California Press, 1959), p. 28.
4. *Works*, vol. II, p. 405.
5. Cf. Baruch Hochman, *The Fiction of S. Y. Agnon* (Ithaca and London: Cornell University Press, 1970), p. 25.

2. *The Abandoned Wife*

1. *Works*, vol. II, p. 405.
2. Ibid., vol. II, p. 415.
3. Cf. A. J. Band, *Nostalgia and Nightmare: A Study in*

the Fiction of S. Y. Agnon (Berkeley and Los Angeles: University of California Press, 1968), pp. 9, 60.
4. *Works*, vol. I, chap. 1, p. 12.
5. The "epic" qualities of Agnon are stressed in the critical writings of Barukh Kurzweil, see especially his *Essays on Agnon's Fiction* [Hebrew] (Tel-Aviv: Schocken, 1970), chap. I, *passim*.
6. *Works*. This is made clear from chap. 14 of the First Book (vol. I, p. 204).
7. *Works*, vol. III, p. 490.

3. *The Childhood Oath*

1. Erich Auerbach, *Scenes from the Drama of European Literature* (New York: Meridian Books, 1959), pp. 11–76.
2. For further discussion, see Harold Fisch, "The Figure of the Dybbuk," *Commentary*, April, 1971, pp. 70–75.
3. Reprinted by permission of Schocken Books Inc. from *Two Tales by S. Y. Agnon*, translated by Walter Lever, copyright © 1966, by Schocken Books Inc., p. 136.
4. Ibid., p. 91.
5. Ibid., pp. 120–21.
6. Ibid., pp. 138–39.
7. Cf. Dov Sadan, *Studies in Agnon* [Hebrew] (Tel-Aviv: Hakkibutz Hameuchad, 1959), pp. 91–94.
8. Lever, *Two Tales by S. Y. Agnon*, p. 166.
9. The emphasis on home and homelessness in this novel is dealt with by Kurzweil, *Essays on Agnon's Fiction*, chap. 1.

4. *The Lost Key*

1. Cf. Arnold Band's impressive study of Agnon: *Nostalgia and Nightmare* (Berkeley and Los Angeles: University of California Press, 1968).
2. See Gershon Shaked, *The Narrative Art of S. Y. Agnon* [Hebrew] (Tel-Aviv: Sifriat Poalim, 1973), p. 228.
3. Ibid., pp. 228–78. The originality in Agnon's use of the first-person narrator in this novel is perceptively discussed by Shaked.
4. *Works*, vol. IV, chap. 6, p. 28.
5. Ibid., vol. IV, chap. 15, p. 76.
6. Ibid., vol. IV, chap. 79, p. 440.
7. See Hochman, *The Fiction of S. Y. Agnon*, p. 139.

5. *Between Dream and Waking*

1. *Works*, vol. IV, chap. 54, p. 308.
2. Cf. Isaiah Rabinovich, *Major Trends in Modern Hebrew Fiction* (Chicago and London: The University of Chicago Press, 1968), p. 204.
3. Ibid., pp. 197, 200, 202.
4. *Works*, vol. IV, chap. 10, p. 43.
5. Ibid., vol. V, p. 126.
6. Lever, *Two Tales by S. Y. Agnon*, p. 84.
7. This formula is evidently based on the initial letters of the Hebrew text of *Song of Songs* 4: 16 ("Let my beloved come to his garden and eat his pleasant fruits."). See M. Tochner, *The Meaning of Agnon* [Hebrew] (Tel-Aviv: Massada, 1968), p. 111.
8. Lever, *Two Tales by S. Y. Agnon*, p. 218.

6. The *Book of Fables*

1. "Fables" is the best rendering of the Hebrew. It is sometimes wrongly translated as "The Book of Deeds."
2. Agnon and Kafka shared many traditions and both of them grew up in the pre-war Austro-Hungarian Empire. On their many affinities, see Hillel Barzel, *Agnon and Kafka: A Comparative Study* [Hebrew] (Israel: Bar-Urian, Ramat-Gan, 1972), *passim.*
3. There is satire here on the naming of names. We could render this Mr. Bigger Little.
4. *Works,* vol. VI, p. 111.
5. Ibid., p. 164.
6. Ibid., p. 168.
7. Ibid., p. 145.
8. Ibid., p. 153.

7. *A Simple Tale*

1. *Works,* vol. III, pp. 92–94.
2. Cf. Ruth R. Wisse, *The Schlemiel as Modern Hero* (Chicago: University of Chicago Press, 1971), pp. 30–57.
3. Cf. Harold Fisch, *The Dual Image: The Figure of the Jew in English and American Literature* (New York: Ktav Publishing House, 1971), pp. 119 f.
4. Wisse, *The Schlemiel as Modern Hero,* p. 53.
5. *Works,* vol. III, p. 272.
6. Ibid., p. 246.
7. The reversal of genders in the relationship of Israel and the *Shekhina* also occurs in the poetry of Agnon's contemporaries C. N. Bialik and A. Shlonsky. See "The Absent God," *Judaism,* vol. XXI (New York, 1972), pp. 415–23.
8. *Works,* vol. III, p. 184.
9. Ibid., p. 227.

8. *Postscript*

1. For a perceptive discussion see Amnon Shamush, *On Agnon's Shira* [Hebrew] (Tel-Aviv: HaHugim Lesifrut, November 1972), p. 16.
2. *Shira* [Hebrew] (Tel-Aviv: Schocken, 1971) book II, chap. 10, pp. 228–29.
3. Cf. Robert Alter, "Agnon's Last Word," *Commentary*, June 1971, pp. 74–81.
4. *Shira*, book II, chap. 11, p. 235.
5. Agnon was at the time critical of the "Peace League" (*Berit Shalom*) headed by Dr. Judah Magnes of the Hebrew University, and dedicated to the idea of a bi-nationalist or federalist solution of the Palestine conflict. This group later on opposed the establishment of an independent Jewish State. Agnon was a no-nonsense Zionist. After the Six-Day War in September 1967, he signed the manifesto of the Land of Israel Movement, the gist of which was that all the territory occupied by the Israeli army in that war was the inalienable possession of the Jewish People and could in no circumstances be ceded to Israel's enemies.
6. *Haaretz* (Tel-Aviv), March 29, 1972.
7. *Shira*, book IV, chap. 8, p. 534.
8. See "Flood Tide" and "A Poet's Continuing Silence" in A. B. Yehoshua's remarkable collection, *Three Days and A Child*, translated by Miriam Arad (New York: Doubleday, 1970).

Bibliography

The works below are a listing of Agnon's major publications in book form. The transliterated Hebrew title with its date of publication is given first, followed by an English title. When a work has been translated into English, date of publication and other pertinent information follows the English title.

Stories and Novels

Agunot, 1908. "Deserted Wives" tr. by Baruch Hochman, *Congress Bi-weekly,* vol. XXXIII, no. 14. (New York, 1966.)

Vehaya He'Akov LeMishor, 1912 (And the Crooked Shall Be Made Straight).

BiLevav Yamin, 1935. *In the Heart of the Seas,* tr. by I. M. Lask. New York: Schocken Books, 1948.

Sippur Pashut, 1935 (A Simple Tale).

Oreah Nata Lalun, 1935. *A Guest for the Night,* tr. by Misha Louvish. New York: Schocken Books, 1968.

Temol Shilshom, 1945 (The Day Before Yesterday).

Shira, 1971 (Shira). A posthumous novel.

BeHanuto shel Mar Lublin, 1974 (In Mr. Lublin's Shop). A posthumous novel.

Collections of Short Stories

Sefer HaMa'asim, 1931; enlarged edition 1951 (Book of Fables). Includes "Pat Shelema," tr. as "A Whole Loaf" by I. M. Lask in a collection of short stories entitled *A Whole Loaf,* ed. by S. J. Kahn. Tel-Aviv, 1957.

Beshuva VeNahat, 1935 (Easy and Quiet). Includes "HaMitpahat," tr. as "The Kerchief" by I. M. Lask which first appeared in a collection entitled *The Jewish Caravan,* ed. by L. J. Schwarz. New York, 1935.

Elu Ve'Elu, 1941 (These and Those). Includes "HaRofe Ugerushato," tr. as "The Doctor's Divorce" by Robert Alter in a collection entitled *Hebrew Short Stories,* ed. by S. Y. Penueli and A. Ukhmani. Tel-Aviv, 1965.

Samukh VeNir'e, 1951 (Near and Visible).

Ad Henna, 1952 (Till Here). Includes "Shevu'at Emunim" and "Ido Ve'Enam," tr. as "Betrothed" and "Edo and Enam" by Walter Lever in *Two Tales by S. Y. Agnon.* New York: Schocken Books, 1966.

Ir UMelo'a, 1973 (A Teeming City). Posthumous stories.

Collected Works

Kol Sippurav shel Sh. Y. Agnon, 4 vols., 1931. The first two volumes contain the full-length novel *Hakhnasat Kala,* tr. by I. M. Lask as *The Bridal Canopy.* New York: Doubleday, 1937.

Kol Sippurav shel Sh. Y. Agnon, 2nd ed., 7 vols., 1953. Volume 8 entitled *Ha'Esh Veha'Etzim* (The Fire and the Wood), a collection of stories, was added in

1962. This is the standard edition of Agnon's complete fiction as published in his lifetime.

Miscellaneous

Yamin Noraim, 1938. *Days of Awe,* tr. by M. T. Galpert, New York: Schocken Books, 1948. Religious meditations and legends.

Atem Re'item, 1959 (You Have Seen). Anthology of Rabbinic sayings and anecdotes.

NOTE: Additional translations are included in *Twenty-One Stories,* ed. by Nahum N. Glatzer. New York: Schocken Books, 1970.

For a detailed list of English translations of Agnon, see: Yohai Goell, *Bibliography of Modern Hebrew Literature in English Translation* (Jerusalem: Israel Universities Press, 1968), pp. 58–60.

Works about Agnon

IN ENGLISH

Band, Arnold J. *Nostalgia and Nightmare: A Study in the Fiction of S. Y. Agnon,* 1968. Contains full bibliography.

Fisch, Harold. "Agnon's Tales of Mystery and Imagination," *Tradition* IX (1967), pp. 123–37.

———. "The Dreaming Narrator in S. Y. Agnon," *Novel* IV (1970), pp. 49–68.

Hochman, Baruch. *The Fiction of S. Y. Agnon,* 1970.

Rabinovich, Isaiah. "Shmuel Yosef Agnon's Techniques of Characterization," *Major Trends in Modern Hebrew Fiction,* 1968.

Wilson, Edmund. "The Fiction of S. Y. Agnon," *Red, Black, Blond and Olive,* 1956.

IN HEBREW

Barzel, Hillel. *Bein Agnon LeKafka: Mehkar Mashve*, 1972.

Kurzweil, Barukh. *Massot al Sippure Shay Agnon*, 1970.

Kurzweil, Barukh, ed. *Yuval Shay*, 1958.

Sadan, Dov. *Al Shay Agnon*, 1959.

Sadan, Dov and Urbach, Efraim, ed. *Le'Agnon Shay: Devarim al HaSofer USefarav*, 1959.

Shaked, Gershon. *Omonut HaSippur shel Agnon*, 1973.

Tochner, Meshullam. *Pesher Agnon*, 1968.

Index